W9-CIB-401

A Learning Ideabook™

Make Your Own Games Workshop by Craig Pearson

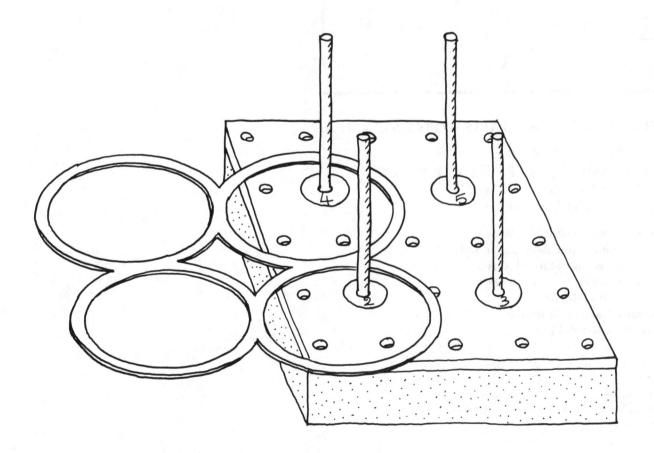

Fearon Teacher Aids, Carthage, Illinois

90707

OTHER TITLES IN THE CRAFTS WORKSHOP SERIES:

INVENTORS WORKSHOP
NATIVE AMERICAN CRAFTS WORKSHOP
NATURE CRAFTS WORKSHOP
TRASH ARTISTS WORKSHOP

Editorial director: Roberta Suid
Editors: Bonnie Bernstein, Zanae Jelletich
Production editor: Mary McClellan
Design manager: Eleanor Mennick
Designer: Jane Mitchell
Illustrator: Jaclyne Scardova
Cover designer: William Nagel

Entire contents copyright ©1982 by Fearon Teacher Aids,
1204 Buchanan Street, P.O. Box 280, Carthage, Illinois 62321.
Permission is hereby granted to reproduce designated
materials in this book for noncommercial classroom and
individual use.

ISBN-0-8224-9782-4
Library of Congress Catalog Card Number: 81-82042
Printed in the United States of America.

1.9 8 7 6 5 4

Contents

Chapter Five
RECYCLED JUNK GAMES 61

GAME SHEETS

Introduction

Make Your Own Games Workshop is a book full of plans and patterns for building more than 30 basic game formats and creating unlimited variations. The activities, which range from high-action games to strategy games, incorporate learning concepts in the fields of math, science, social studies, and language arts, along with some physical challenges. All in all, they're fun and educational for kids aged 9 and up—and older kids and adults will find many of them interesting and challenging as well.

The **Workshop** games are primarily intended to act as a springboard for original game designs. In addition to step-by-step directions and rules for play, each game includes suggestions for adapting the basic format to create new variations or to invent an entirely new game. By mixing and matching ideas and materials, revising the content, or rewriting rules, kids will discover unlimited game possibilities.

Most **Workshop** games can be put together in well under an hour; in fact, some formats are featured on game sheets (found in the back of the book) that can be duplicated and ready for play in minutes. The construction of each game requires only simple tools and readily available materials—household mainstays and recyclable throwaways—which makes the games ideal for kids working independently at home or in the classroom.

THE ANTHROPOLOGY OF GAMES

Game making is a wonderful, basic human ability. People made games long before they learned to write. Dozens of games that remain popular today, from hopscotch and jacks to backgammon and chess, are over 2,000 to 3,000 years old. Game boards and playing pieces have been excavated from the ruins of ancient cities in Egypt, the old Roman and Greek empires, and many other parts of the world. The exact origins of these games probably date back even further.

Games are as widespread as they are old. They have existed in most of the world's cultures, from the richest and most powerful to the simplest tribal societies. And the kinds of games played by very different peoples in very different places show remarkable similarities. Often, only the native materials available for making the playing pieces change from one culture to the next.

Many games today are just for fun, but in the past most societies intentionally designed games to develop practical skills in farming, fishing, hunting, and warfare, and to instruct their people in the rules and traditions of family life, religion, and culture. Indeed, some historians believe that making games helped people learn how to make laws and rules of fair play for their societies.

The integrity of games lies in their inherent simplicity and in human ingenuity. The earliest games consisted of playing pieces provided by nature, such as pebbles, shells, twigs, and bones, and were played on primitive gameboards—lines or pockets scratched in the ground. Some of these games, such as Japanese *Go* and African *Mancala*, are so full of playing possibilities that even today, centuries after they were first invented, new ideas about them are still being written and discussed. Even with the advent of electronic games, it is the simple games that have endured and claim the greatest popularity, such as checkers and dominoes. And despite fancy prepackaging of most games today, kids and adults continue spontaneously to devise entertaining and often challenging games from whatever material is at hand. A wad of paper and a fried chicken bucket, for example, have been known to turn into an exciting version of basketball.

GAMES AS TOOLS OF LEARNING

Most of the games in *Make Your Own Games Workshop* incorporate basic learning skills or concepts in at least one of the major curricular areas. Many of the game projects have a Variations section that includes suggestions for adapting the games to focus on more than one skill or discipline. This allows kids to bone up on their fundamental skills and have fun at the same time. In fact, games have proven to be an effective learning tool for kids who have had difficulty with other, more traditional, learning approaches.

Not only do the *Workshop* games reinforce learning skills and concepts through play, but they also incorporate chance, competition, strategy, and physical challenges in various proportions. Playing a game that relies entirely on chance gives players no opportunity to develop skills. On the other hand, a game that is entirely competitive can emphasize defeating an opponent rather than achieving individual skills. To avoid such one-sidedness, the games in this book have been designed to balance chance, competition, and skills and strategy in productive ways.

MATERIALS AND TOOLS FOR GAMES

Be creative and imaginative when selecting materials for constructing *Workshop* games. The objective is to move away from prepackaged new games that leave little to the imagination toward games that can be built from scratch out of readily available materials—materials that can be found in most households or purchased inexpensively.

Though tools used in constructing the games are simple, safety considerations should not be ignored. Surprisingly, however, sharp tools, such as matte knives, often are safer than dull ones for cutting cardboard or making interior cuts in paper, so don't rule them out altogether. A sharp instrument is less likely to slip than a dull one, and it works more efficiently. A good precautionary measure for using a cutting instrument is to wear a heavy glove on the hand that's not holding the instrument. Small manicure scissors are useful for making interior cuts in paper. Another cutting tool that's both useful and safe is the plastic Coupon Cutter, manufactured by Tru-Bilt, which can be found at many variety and discount stores.

Use the lists of Recyclable Materials, Household Materials, and Tools to set up a game-making workshop at home or at school.

Recyclable Materials

Aluminum foil paper, tins, or trays
Cardboard circles from pizzas or cakes
Cardboard tubes from paper rolls
Cardboard backing from shirts or pads of
    paper
Cereal boxes
Corks
Egg cartons
Gift boxes, especially shirt boxes
    (about 2 inches deep, 9 inches wide,
    and 12 inches long)
Jar lids
Bottle caps (metal or plastic)
Corrugated light bulb packaging
Milk cartons

Newspapers
Paper bags
Cylindrical shakers for grated cheese or
    spices
Spout containers for salt or bread
    crumbs
String
Styrofoam packing material (solid sheets
    or "peanuts")
Thread spools
Tin cans
Twist ties and plastic fasteners
Wrapping paper (plain brown) or news-
    print

Household Materials

Adhesive vinyl paper scraps
Ball bearings
Balls, small rubber or Ping-Pong
Beads
Bingo chips and other game markers
Buttons (large and flat)
Cellophane tape
Dried beans (various colors and shapes)
Drinking straws
Erasers
Glue (stick, model, or epoxy)
Golf tees
Graph paper
Hole reinforcements for notebook paper

Jar rings for canning
Marbles
Masking tape
Nails
Nuts and bolts
Paper clips
Paper plates
Pasta alphabet letters and numbers
Pegboard (scrap pieces)
Rubber bands
Washers (metal, plastic, and rubber)
Wood dowels
Wood or plywood scraps

Tools

Can openers (punch and standard types)
Compass
Coupon Cutter
Drill with $5/32$-inch drill bit
Felt-tip markers and pens
Hammer
Matte knife
Paper punch
Ruler

Sandpaper
Scissors (manicure and standard)
Screwdriver
Small saw (such as coping saw, saber
    saw, or hack saw)
Stapler
Utility knife
Yardstick

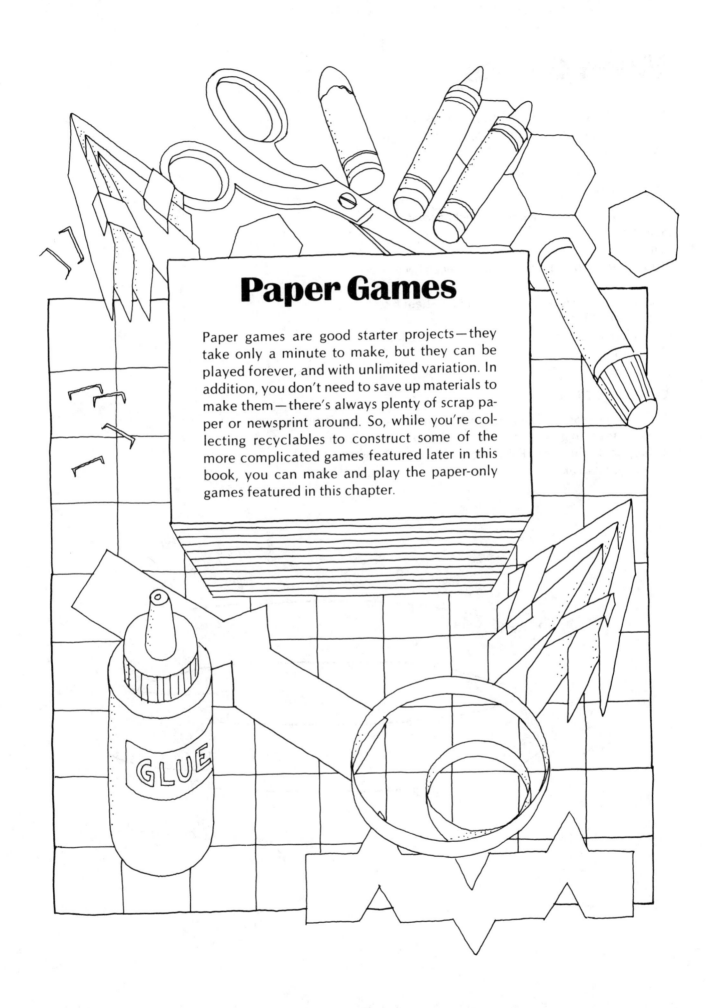

Paper Games

Paper games are good starter projects—they take only a minute to make, but they can be played forever, and with unlimited variation. In addition, you don't need to save up materials to make them—there's always plenty of scrap paper or newsprint around. So, while you're collecting recyclables to construct some of the more complicated games featured later in this book, you can make and play the paper-only games featured in this chapter.

GLUE

Word Quoits

The target looks like a jumble, but a toss of the quoit helps players build reading skills for high word scores.

MATERIALS AND TOOLS

Strip of paper, 1 inch wide, 8½ inches long
Scissors
Glue
Word Find Quoits Target (Game Sheet #1 on
  page 76)
Word Scramble Quoits Target (Game Sheet #2
  on page 77)
Scratch pad or paper
Pencil

CONSTRUCTION

1. Cut out the strip of paper. Cover ½ inch at one end of the paper strip with glue. Join the ends to make a loop, or *quoit*.
2. Duplicate the Word Find Quoits Target and the Word Scramble Quoits Target.

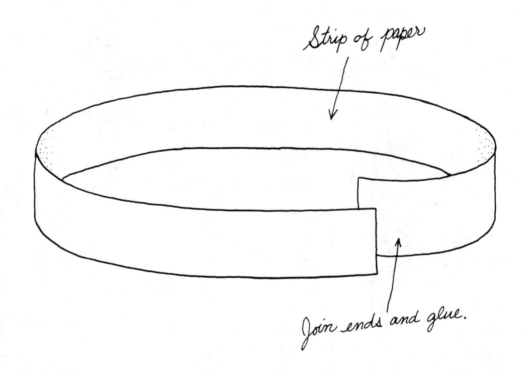

Strip of paper

Join ends and glue.

HOW TO PLAY WORD FIND QUOITS *(2 to 4 players)*

1. Lay the target on the floor or on a table. The first player holds the quoit 6 inches away from the page, and then tosses it onto the page. The quoit should land flat on the target. If it doesn't, the player tries again until it does land flat.
2. The player has 15 seconds to read all the words, left to right and top to bottom, that show completely inside the quoit. For example, the player who tossed the quoit on the target pictured here reads *AT, TO, PEN, EVE, EVER,* and *LEVER* from left to right, and *APE, PET,* and *ONE* from top to bottom.
3. The player writes down all the words and scores 1 point for each letter in each word. In the example, the score for the turn is 28.
4. Players take turns until one player wins with a score of 100.

HOW TO PLAY WORD SCRAMBLE QUOITS *(2 to 4 players)*

1. Lay the target on the floor or on a table. The first player tosses the quoit onto the target, as in Word Find Quoits.
2. When the quoit has landed flat on the page, the player has 15 seconds to make as many words as possible from any of the letters that show inside the quoit. For example, the player who tossed the quoit on the target pictured here might scramble letters to make the words *LIKE, ONE, TEN, TON, NET,* or *RIG.* But there's a bigger score to be had for *GRIT, TIRE,* or *RING,* and a bigger score yet for *TIGER.*
3. The player writes down all the words and scores 1 point for each letter in each word.
4. Players take turns until one player wins with a score of 50.

■ VARIATIONS

1. Allow either more or less time for a player to read or scramble words. If you allow more time, play for a higher winning score. If you allow less time, play for a lower winning score.
2. Make a new word target that allows a player to find or make more words and bigger words (this can be done for either game). Include more than the original number of letters, and make the letters smaller so that they fit the target. Be sure to use plenty of vowels and to arrange the words for Word Find Quoits so that they overlap.

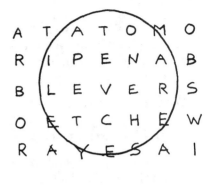

AT	2
TO	2
PEN	3
EVE	3
EVER	4
LEVER	5
APE	3
PET	3
ONE	3

28 points

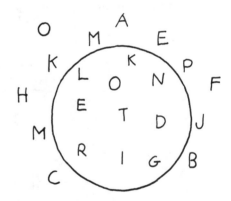

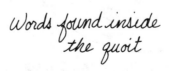

Words found inside the quoit

TIRE	4
TIGER	5
RING	4
LIKE	4
ONE	3
TEN	3
TON	3
NET	3
RIG	3
GRIT	4

36 points

Number Quoits

This game challenges players to sharpen calculating skills without the benefit of a pencil and paper. Begin with an easy but fast-moving version. Then make the game more difficult as players' skills grow.

MATERIALS AND TOOLS

2 strips of paper, 1 inch wide, 8½ inches long
1 strip of paper, 1 inch wide, 4 inches long
Scissors
Glue
Number Quoits Target (Game Sheet #3 on page 78)

CONSTRUCTION

1. Cut out the strips of paper. Apply glue to one end of each paper strip, covering about ½ inch. Join the ends together to make three separate loops, or quoits.
2. Glue the smaller loop to the inside of one of the larger loops (see illustration). This is called a double quoit.
3. Duplicate the Number Quoits Target.

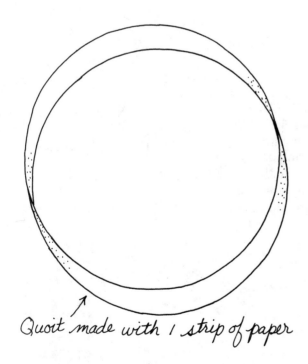

Quoit made with 1 strip of paper

Quoit made with 2 strips of paper

HOW TO PLAY WITH THE SINGLE QUOIT (2 to 4 players)

1. Lay the target on the floor or on a table. The first player holds the single quoit 6 inches away from the page and tosses it onto the page. The quoit should land flat. If it doesn't, the player tosses again until it does land flat.
2. The player has 10 seconds to add up all the numbers that show completely inside the quoit. If a number shows only partially, it is not counted.
3. The other player(s) checks the total within 10 seconds. If it is correct, the sum counts as the first player's score for the turn. If the total is incorrect, the second player subtracts 5 from the sum and takes the difference as his or her score.
4. Players take turns until one player wins with a score of 200.

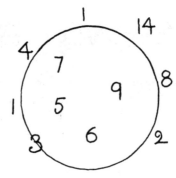

Score =27

HOW TO PLAY WITH THE DOUBLE QUOIT (2 to 4 players)

1. Lay the target on the floor or on a table. The first player tosses the double quoit onto the target just as he or she would toss the single quoit.
2. When the double quoit has landed flat on the page, the player has 20 seconds to add up all the numbers that show completely inside the larger loop of the double quoit, then subtract any number that shows completely inside the smaller loop.
3. Only correct answers score. The number of points a player wins in a turn is equal to the final answer the player arrives at after adding and subtracting. Players take turns until one player wins with a score of 200.

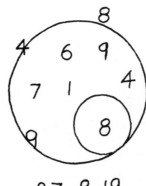

27−8=19

■ VARIATIONS

1. Players use larger or smaller quoits for either game, and larger or smaller numbers on their own made-up targets. The time limit for a turn is varied accordingly: If larger quoits or smaller numbers are used, players increase the time; if smaller quoits or larger numbers are used, players decrease the time.
2. If players are using the single quoit, they can multiply rather than add all the numbers that show inside the quoit, playing to a score of 1,000. If players are using the double quoit, they can add up all the numbers that show completely inside the larger loop of the double quoit, then multiply that sum by any number that shows completely inside the smaller loop. Players play to a score of 500.

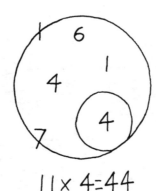

11 x 4=44

3. If players are using the double quoit, they can add up all the numbers that show completely inside the larger loop of the double quoit, then divide that sum by any number that shows completely inside the smaller loop of the quoit. Players play to a score of 100, rounding up or down to the nearest whole number when necessary.

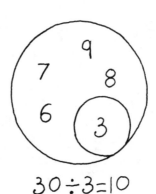

30÷3=10

Flying Word Find

This game combines both word-building skills and motor skills. Once players learn to pilot the flying pointer, they can land all kinds of words on the big target.

MATERIALS AND TOOLS

3 strips of paper, 7 inches long and 2 inches wide (for floor play) or 3½ inches long and 1 inch wide (for desk play)
Scissors
Sheet of paper, 3 feet square (for floor play) or 18 inches square (for desk play)
Black felt-tip pen

CONSTRUCTION

1. Cut the strips of paper into three flying pointers exactly like the one shown here. Decorate them any way you like.
2. Divide the large sheet of paper into 81 4-inch squares. Transfer the small target pattern shown here to the paper.

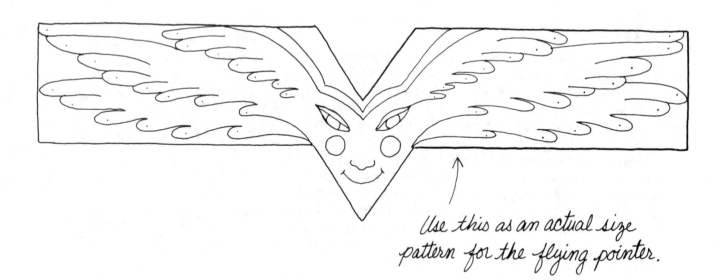

Use this as an actual size pattern for the flying pointer.

HOW TO PLAY (4 players)

1. Lay the target on the floor. Each player uses all three flying pointers each turn, releasing them from waist height or higher. Players can pilot the pointers in any manner they wish. They can release the pointers one at a time, or two or three at a time, and from a point directly over the target or several feet away from the target. Players should decide in advance whether or not a pointer that misses the target completely can be played again.

2. Players score 5 points for any word made in one turn from the word parts on the target that are touched by the flying pointers. For example, the pointers in the illustration are touching BR and ING; the player scores 5 points for the word BRING. A player scores 15 points for any word made of three parts touched by the pointers, such as TH INK ING or IN ST EAD.

3. The first player to score 50 points wins.

■ VARIATION

Players can store up all the word parts they get by writing them down. They can then combine word parts from various turns. Award 5 points for each two-part word and 10 points for each three-part word.

CH	Y	SL	AMP	CL	USH	CR	UNK	SP
ORE	THR	IN	WH	ART	SK	OSE	G L	ING
PR	ARE	DR	OW	GR	INK	SCR	OKE	SL
ILL	STR	ASH	TH	IP	BR	AP	SW	EAK
FR	ALL	SHR	AIN	FL	EAM	TR	IME	DR
AY	BL	UM	SM	EW	ST	EAT	PL	ASH
SPL	EAR	GL	IM	SP	AND	SPR	ACK	PR
OVE	GR	INE	CH	Y	CL	EAD	SN	AT
BR	UB	ST	OWN	DR	OT	SQU	OP	TR

3-foot-square target pattern

Target pattern is made of 4-inch squares.

Whole in One

This game gives players a chance to try their math skills in adding both like and unlike fractions. The triple-pointed flyers can be expertly guided to land on fractions that can be combined into whole numbers.

MATERIALS AND TOOLS

2 strips of paper, 7 inches long and 3 inches
    wide (for floor play) or 3½ inches long and
    1½ inches wide (for desk play)
Scissors
Sheet of paper, 3 feet square (for floor play) or
    18 inches square (for desk play)
Black felt-tip pen

CONSTRUCTION

1. Cut the strips of paper into two triple-pointed flyers exactly like the one shown here. Decorate them any way you like.
2. Divide the large sheet of paper into 81 4-inch squares. Transfer the small target pattern shown here to the paper.

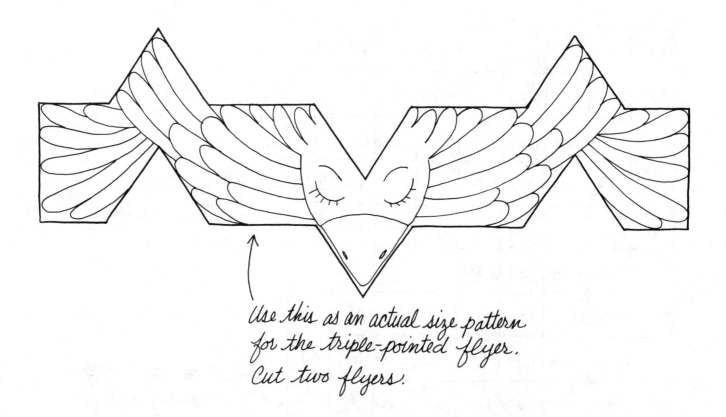

Use this as an actual size pattern for the triple-pointed flyer. Cut two flyers.

HOW TO PLAY (4 players)

1. Lay the target on the floor. Each player uses both flying pointers for every turn. Pointers must be released from waist height or higher, but players can pilot them from any desired position, releasing them either one at a time or both at once. Players should decide in advance whether or not a pointer that misses the target completely can be played again.

2. Players score 1 point for each whole number 1 they make from fractions touched by the six points on the two triple-pointed flyers. For example, if one pointer hits $3/8$, $3/16$, and $1/4$, and the other pointer hits $13/16$, $5/8$, and $1/2$, the player can score 1 point for $5/8 + 3/8$ and 1 point for $13/16 + 3/16$. The $1/2$ and $3/4$ are left over and do not count. Players must keep an eye open for unlike fractions that add up to 1, such as $9/16 + 5/16 + 1/8$ or $1/16 + 3/16 + 1/8 + 1/4 + 3/8$.

3. The first player to score 10 points is the winner.

■ VARIATIONS

1. Players store up all the fractions they get by writing them down. Players combine all their own turns to add fractions. The first player to score 20 points wins.

2. Multiply the two largest fractions together, or subtract the smallest fraction from the next smallest. Correct answers get 1 point. The first player to score 10 points wins.

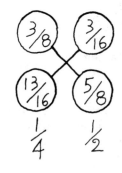

Player's score : 2 points

1/4	1/16	1/8	1/16	1/2	7/8	1/4	1/2	1/16
9/16	5/8	1/2	15/16	3/16	1/2	13/16	7/8	1/2
1/8	11/16	3/4	1/4	1/2	3	1/4	5/16	3/4
1/2	1/4	3/8	1/2	3/4	1/2	5/8	3/4	7/8
1/4	7/16	1/2	5/16	1/8	15/16	7/8	9/16	1/2
3/8	1/2	11/16	3/8	15/16	1/2	13		16
7/16	3/4	1/2	15/16	1/8	7/16	1/4	9/16	1/2
1/4	1/8	3/4	1/2	3/4	7/8	1/2	3/4	5/16
5/8	3/16	1/2	3/8	13/16	1/2	11/16	5/8	1/2

← 3-foot-square target

← Target pattern is made of 4-inch squares.

Puff Grand Prix

This game challenges players' knowledge of various subjects by having them answer Pit Stop questions. An expert may be able to zoom through the whole race course without a halt, but most drivers will find trouble along the way. They will need to use their learning skills to make Pit Stop decisions.

MATERIALS AND TOOLS

3 strips of paper for each racer, 1 inch wide and 8 inches long
40 scraps of paper for Pit Stop questions, about 2 inches square
Glue or stapler
Color markers
Scissors
Sheet of paper for each race track, about 11 inches wide and 3 feet long
Black felt-tip pen

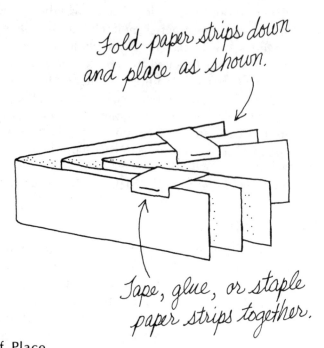

Fold paper strips down and place as shown.

Tape, glue, or staple paper strips together.

CONSTRUCTION

1. To build the racer, fold the three paper strips in half. Place them one inside the other, like Vs inside Vs. Each should be about 1 inch behind the other.
2. Staple or glue each end about ½ inch from the ends of the first V, as shown.
3. Decorate each racer with color markers. Include a racing number, fenders, and wheels. Trim each racer with scissors to complete body designs.
4. Draw a track about 4 inches wide and as long as the large sheet of paper. Make gentle curves and narrow bottlenecks in the track.
5. Players write 20 math, science, social studies, music, art, or language arts questions on their own 20 Pit Stop slips.

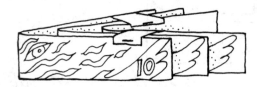

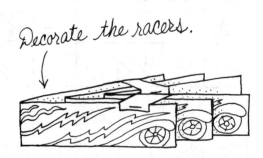

Decorate the racers.

14

HOW TO PLAY (2 players)

1. Players place the tracks side by side, and place the racers on the start line of each track.
2. Each player places the 20 Pit Stop slips alongside the other player's track. The slips are placed facedown and pinned in any position the players choose.
3. At the go signal, players try to puff their racers from the Start to the Finish. Players must stay behind the Start line as they puff.
4. When a player's racer touches a Pit Stop slip, the player must pick up that slip and answer the question correctly before continuing the race. If the player cannot answer the top question, the player must continue through the pile until he or she answers a question correctly. A player who cannot answer any of the questions at a Pit Stop must move back to the preceding Pit Stop and try to answer a question there.
5. The first player to cross the finish line is the winner.

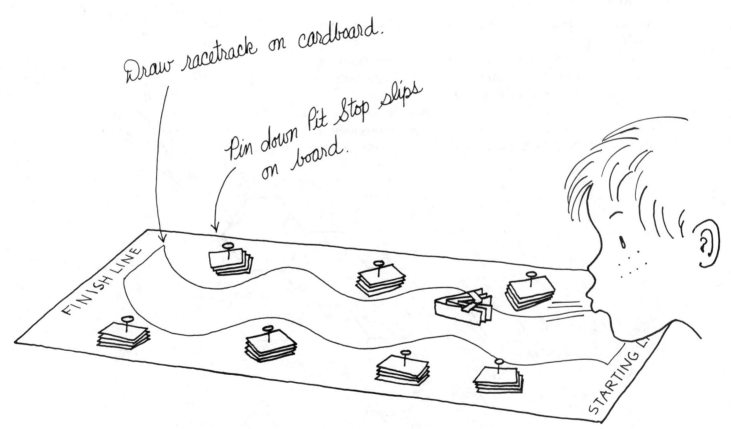

Draw racetrack on cardboard.

Pin down Pit Stop slips on board.

Hex Tens

The assembled honeycomb design in this game looks easy when you prepare it, but once you take it apart, watch out—putting the hexagons together again to make tens can be a tough challenge. The game offers practice in simple calculation, but also gives players experience in the higher math skills of spatial perception and strategy.

MATERIALS AND TOOLS

Sheet of white or brown wrapping paper, at
   least 15 inches square
Hexagon Pattern (Game Sheet #4 on page 79)
Scissors
Black felt-tip pen

CONSTRUCTION

1. Duplicate the Hexagon Pattern, then carefully cut out a 3-inch hexagon.
2. Use the pattern to trace a honeycomb of 20 hexagons, as shown in the illustration. Double or triple the pattern for more players or for a longer game.
3. Fill in the numbers as shown. (Notice that the numbers total 10 at every point where the sides of the hexagons meet.)
4. Cut all the hexagons apart. Then shuffle them into a deck.

Cut all the hexagons apart.

Numbers total 10 where sides meet.

HOW TO PLAY *(2 players)*

1. To start the game, take the first four hexagons from the top of the deck. Place these hexagons in a line in the center of the playing surface so that the touching sides all total 10:

2. Place the rest of the deck facedown. Each player, in turn, draws one hexagon from the deck. The hexagon must be played into the honeycomb on the playing surface.

3. The player scores 1 point for each sum of 10 that is made by joining the sides of the hexagon to others in the pattern. The player can always match one side to make 10, but may not be able to match two or more sides. The object is to find opportunities for moves that can score 2 or more points. At the start, one move can score 1 or 2 points. As the game continues, however, the player may be able to score 3, 4, 5, or even 6 points in one move.

4. The player who has the most points after all the hexagons have been played is the winner.

◼ VARIATIONS

1. Hex Tens can also be played as a solitaire puzzle. The player can use any hexagon in any order. Solutions may differ from the original model, but in all cases at least two sides of every hexagon in the solution must touch the sides of other hexagons. Solitaire players can compare scores with one another over a period of time to see who can get the most hexagons into a perfect 10 pattern.

2. Draw new honeycombs and set up many variations of hexagon numbers games. For example, create one in which all sides meet to form the key numbers 9, 11, 13, and 15. Create another in which the numbers on meeting sides can be multiplied to equal 24, 36, or 48. Be sure to make a copy of your creation before you cut it apart, or you may find it is very difficult to put back together again.

This is how to start the game.

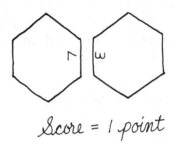

Score = 1 point

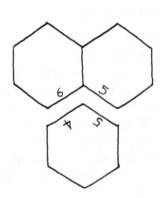

Score = 2 points

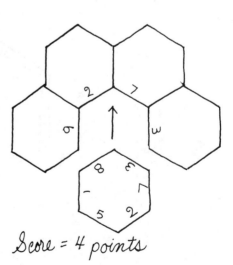

Score = 4 points

Hex-A-Tour

This honeycomb game takes players traveling around the world. Can they combine a knowledge of geography and pattern-matching skills to get top scores?

MATERIALS AND TOOLS

Sheet of paper, 8½ inches wide and 11 inches long
Hexagon Pattern (Game Sheet #4 on page 79)
Scissors
Black felt-tip pen

CONSTRUCTION

1. Duplicate the Hexagon Pattern, then carefully cut out a 2½-inch hexagon.
2. Use the pattern to trace a honeycomb of 10 hexagons, as shown in the illustration. Double or triple the pattern for more players or for a longer game.
3. Fill in the names of cities and countries, as shown. (Notice that, at every side where the hexagons meet, cities are matched to the countries in which they are found.)
4. Cut all the hexagons apart and shuffle them into a deck.

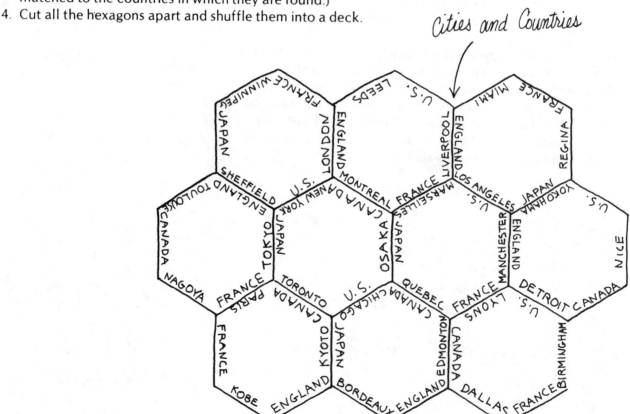

Cities and Countries

HOW TO PLAY *(2 players)*

1. To begin, take the first two hexagons from the top of the deck and place them faceup in the center of the playing surface so the touching side matches one city with the country to which it belongs.

2. Spread the remaining hexagons faceup on the playing surface. Each player, in turn, picks one hexagon and plays it into the honeycomb pattern. The player gets 1 point for each correct match of city to country. The player who has the most points when all the hexagons have been played is the winner.

■ VARIATIONS

Make new honeycomb designs, such as the following, or create your own hexagon games using any subject matter elements that match or equal each other. Just be sure that there are at least two examples of every match or equation in the game.

1. Here is the beginning of a word picture hexagon game. Study the pattern carefully and expand it with more words and pictures. Other reading and language arts hexagon games might use rhyming words, synonyms, or book titles and authors.

Word Picture Game

2. Here is the beginning of an animal-vegetable-mineral hexagon game. Expand it by filling in more hexagons. Write *Animal*, *Vegetable*, and *Mineral* on each hexagon, and include one example from each category on each hexagon.

3. Here is the beginning of an equations hexagon game. Expand it by filling in more hexagons.

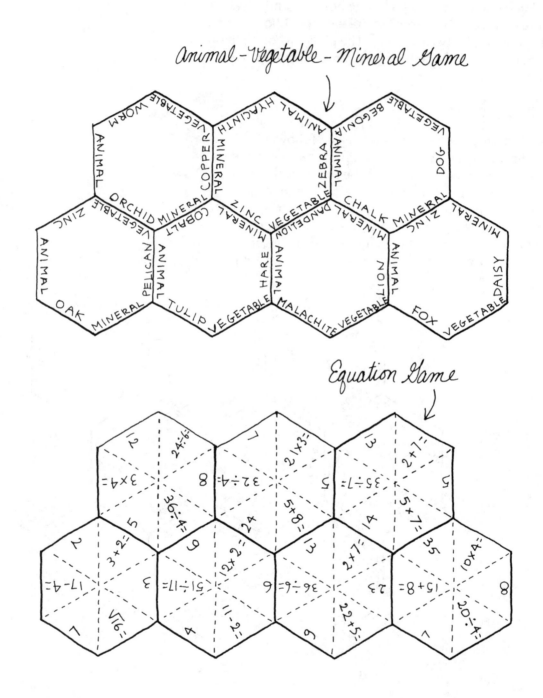

Animal-Vegetable-Mineral Game

Equation Game

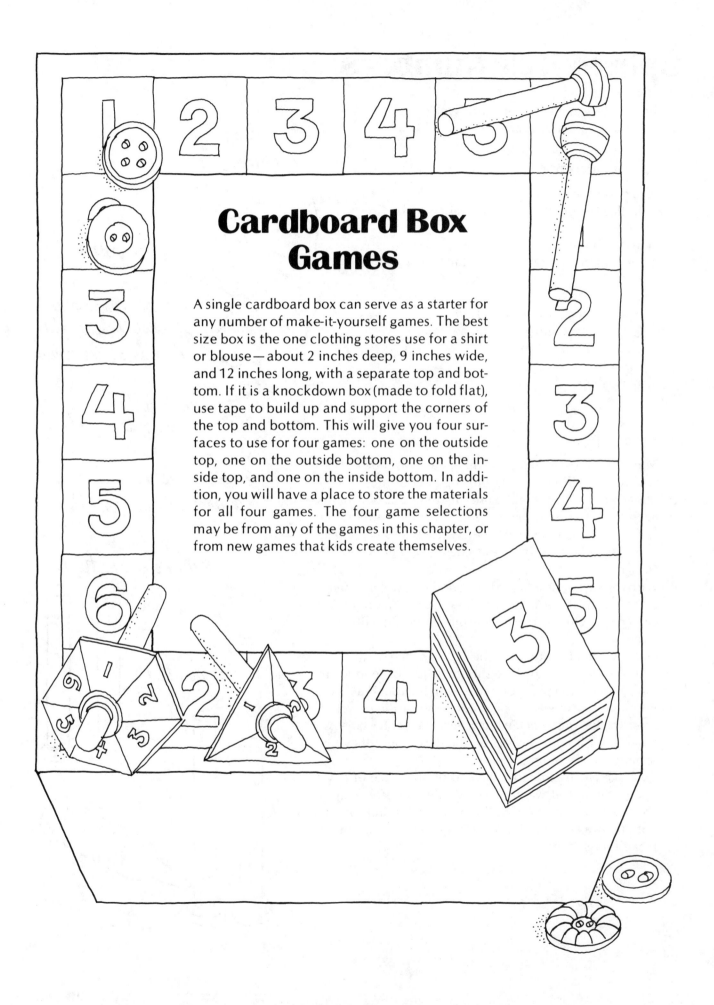

Cardboard Box Games

A single cardboard box can serve as a starter for any number of make-it-yourself games. The best size box is the one clothing stores use for a shirt or blouse—about 2 inches deep, 9 inches wide, and 12 inches long, with a separate top and bottom. If it is a knockdown box (made to fold flat), use tape to build up and support the corners of the top and bottom. This will give you four surfaces to use for four games: one on the outside top, one on the outside bottom, one on the inside top, and one on the inside bottom. In addition, you will have a place to store the materials for all four games. The four game selections may be from any of the games in this chapter, or from new games that kids create themselves.

Spin Skittle Numbers

A whirling teetotum and four skittles make this a lively math operations game.

MATERIALS AND TOOLS

Box top or bottom
Spin Skittle Number Pattern (Game Sheet #5 on
    page 80)
Black felt-tip pen
Teetotum Spinner Pattern (Game Sheet #6 on
    page 81)
Scissors
3-inch-square piece of cardboard
Dowel, 3/16 inch in diameter, 10 inches long
Small saw or pruning shears
Sandpaper
6 faucet washers
Glue

CONSTRUCTION

1. Duplicate the Spin Skittle Number Pattern. Glue it thoroughly to the inside of your box top or bottom.
2. Duplicate the Teetotum Spinner Pattern. Cut out the six-sided teetotum from the pattern. Trace the pattern onto the cardboard square, marking the center by pushing a pencil through the hole. Number the sides 1 through 6 with the felt-tip pen.
3. With the saw or pruning shears, cut the dowel into five pieces, each about 1 3/4 inches long. Sand smooth the ends of each piece. On one piece only, make the end a little rounded.
4. Make a small hole through the center of the cardboard teetotum spinner. The hole should be just big enough to push through the piece of dowel with the rounded end.
5. Push one faucet washer onto each end of the dowel. Put a drop of glue onto each washer near the center hole. Continue to push both washers on the dowel until they rest against the teetotum spinner.
6. To make each skittle, put the end of one piece of dowel into one of the faucet washers. The skittle then stands up, with the faucet washer forming the base. Add a drop of glue to hold the washer and the dowel together. Use this method to make four skittles.

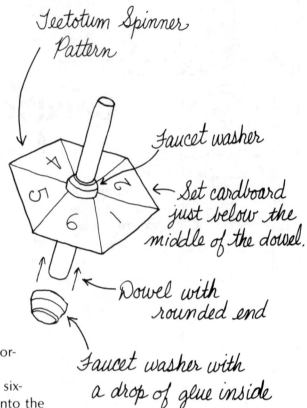

Teetotum Spinner Pattern

Faucet washer

Set cardboard just below the middle of the dowel.

Dowel with rounded end

Faucet washer with a drop of glue inside

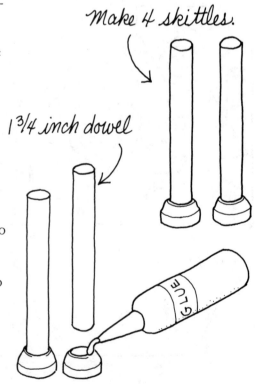

Make 4 skittles.

1 3/4 inch dowel

GLUE

HOW TO PLAY (2 or more players)

1. Set one skittle on each of the + marks.
2. Put the end of the teetotum spinner in the ⊕ box and spin it.
3. When the teetotum stops, multiply the number on the down side (the side resting on the box) by the number in the box it touches. (If it touches two or more boxes, use the lowest number.)
4. Add the number touched by the top end of any knocked-down skittle.
5. Players take turns until one wins with 100 points.

■ **VARIATIONS**

1. If more than two skittles are knocked down, cut the player's score in half.
2. If the end of a knocked-down skittle touches the ⊕ box, double the player's score.

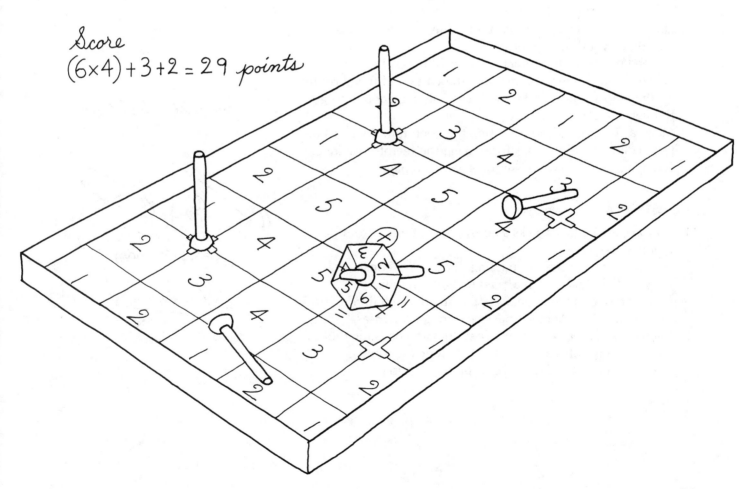

Score
(6×4) + 3 + 2 = 29 points

U.S.A.

This game familiarizes players with many cities and routes around the nation. Which player will be the first to go from border to border or from coast to coast?

MATERIALS AND TOOLS

Box top or bottom
U.S.A. Map Pattern (Game Sheet #7 on page 82)
Glue
Sharp-pointed nail or awl
Teetotum Spinner Pattern (Game Sheet #6 on
    page 81)
Scissors
Piece of cardboard 3 inches square
Dowel, $^3/_{16}$ inch in diameter, $1^3/_4$ inches long
2 faucet washers
Plastic toothpicks, 1 for each player (a different
    color for each)

CONSTRUCTION

1. Duplicate the U.S.A. Map Pattern. Glue it thoroughly to the outside of your box top or bottom.
2. Use the nail or awl to punch very small holes through the center of each large dot, marking the cities and travel routes on the map surface. Make the holes only big enough to go through the box.
3. Make a five-sided teetotum using the Teetotum Spinner Pattern. Follow the directions for making the teetotum spinner given in the Spin Skittle Numbers game on page 22.

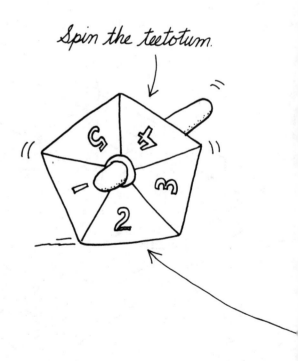

Spin the teetotum.

HOW TO PLAY (2 to 4 players)

1. To start, each player picks a coast-to-coast route from among four possibilities:
   A. Anchorage to Boston, passing through Wisconsin;
   B. Seattle to Philadelphia, passing through Iowa;
   C. Richmond to San Francisco, passing through Illinois; or
   D. Miami to Los Angeles, passing through Arkansas.
2. Each player, in turn, spins the teetotum and pegs the toothpick as many holes as are indicated along the route.
3. The first player to finish the coast-to-coast trip wins.

■ VARIATIONS

1. Try scoring another way. Each player who lands exactly in a city at the end of a spin gets 1 point. The first player to go coast-to-coast gets 10 points, the second player 9 points, the third player 8 points, and the fourth player 7 points. The player who finishes with the most points wins.

2. Add your own home town and other familiar places to the map. See who can visit the most states in 10 turns, or who can go through the fewest states on a trip from Alaska to Florida, or from Hawaii to Massachusetts.

3. Try the Mystery Tour. To begin, each player makes up a secret list of any 10 cities on the map. (The cities can be close together or far apart.) If there are two players, each of them makes this secret list for the other player to complete. If more than two are playing, each player makes this list for the player to the left. A player can start from any city on the map. Each player spins the teetotum every turn and moves the number of steps shown. Every time a player lands on a city or passes through it, that player must be told if the city is on his or her secret list. The first player to visit or pass through all 10 cities on the secret list is the winner.

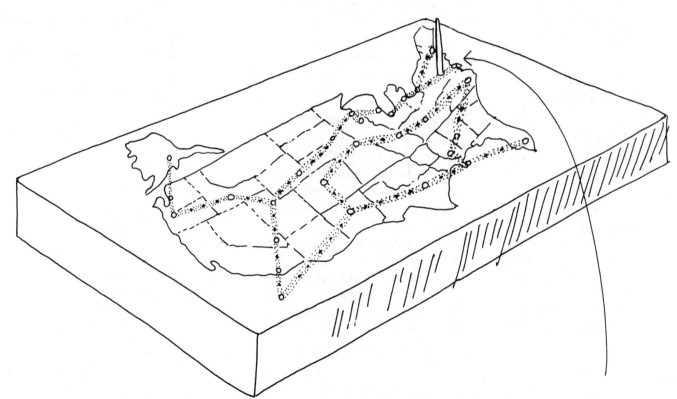

The 2 means place the toothpick in the second hole of the route.

Animal Hunt

Players in this game get acquainted with more than 30 animals and their names, and strive to capture 10.

Glue Animal Hunt Pattern inside box.

MATERIALS AND TOOLS

Box top or bottom
Animal Hunt Pattern (Game sheet #8 on
   page 83)
Glue
1-inch cube of Styrofoam

CONSTRUCTION

Duplicate the Animal Hunt Pattern. Glue it thoroughly to the inside of your box top or bottom.

HOW TO PLAY *(2 to 4 players)*

1. Each player, in turn, puts the Styrofoam cube on the Animal Hunt square in the center and moves it with just one puff.
2. The player captures the animals in the square on which the Styrofoam cube lands. If the cube touches two, three, or four squares, the player captures all animals in those squares.
3. The first player to capture 10 animals wins the game.

■ VARIATIONS

1. Before the game begins, each player secretly writes down the names of two of the animals. If there are two players, the secret animals cannot be captured and held by the other player. If there are more than two players, the secret animals cannot be captured and held by the player to the left. If the player captures one of these animals, the animal then escapes, leading three other animals away with it. Once the animal escapes, the player can write down the name of the same secret animal or another secret animal.
2. Adapt the game form to other subjects. For example, players may try to capture several books by the same author, several words with the same prefix, several multiples of the same number, or several cities in the same state.

Shopping List

This board game encourages players to budget their resources, seek out best buys, and try out bargaining skills.

MATERIALS AND TOOLS

Box top or bottom
Shopping List Pattern (Game Sheet #9 on page 84)
Glue
Teetotum Spinner Pattern (Game Sheet #6 on page 81)
Scissors
Piece of cardboard 3 inches square
Dowel, $3/16$ inch in diameter, $1^3/4$ inches long
2 faucet washers
Buttons for plastic tabs for markers

CONSTRUCTION

1. Duplicate the Shopping List Pattern. Glue it thoroughly to the outside of the box.
2. Make a three-sided teetotum, using the Teetotum Spinner Pattern. Follow the directions given in the Spin Skittle Numbers game on page 22.

HOW TO PLAY (2 to 4 players)

1. Each player has an account of $200. Before beginning the game, each player makes out a secret shopping list of 10 items displayed on the game board. At least five of these items must have a purchase price above $10.
2. Players put their markers in the Start square. Players may stay in the outside track or may move into the inside squares at any one of the four entry points. Moves on the outside track must be counterclockwise. Moves in the inside squares may be made in any direction, as long as the player does not enter a square twice in the same turn.
3. A player who lands in a square may buy the product shown in that square, at the price listed. Any other player, however, may bid up the price in whole-dollar increments. The highest bidder gets to buy the product.
4. The first player to reach the Finish square must pay an exit fee of $5. The second player must pay $10, the third player $15, and the fourth player $20.
5. The player who finishes the game with the most purchases from his or her secret shopping list—and without overspending the $200 account—is the winner.

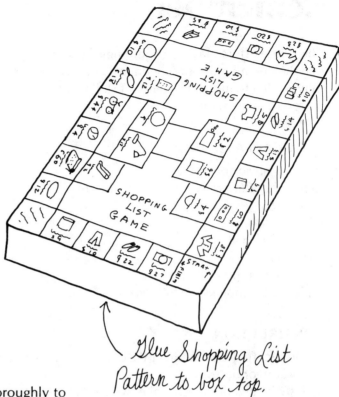

Glue Shopping List Pattern to box top.

Use buttons for markers.

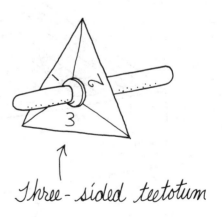

Three-sided teetotum

Remember

This game offers players a challenge: how well can they recall number sequences? High scores may be due to luck, but plenty of skill is required to make them count.

MATERIALS AND TOOLS

Box top or bottom
Remember Pattern (Game Sheet #10 on
   page 85)
Glue
Awl or thin nail
10 file cards
Black felt-tip pen
4 plastic toothpicks, each a different color

CONSTRUCTION

1. Duplicate the Remember Pattern. Glue it thoroughly to the box top or bottom.
2. Use the awl or nail to make two small holes at each number on the game surface. Just barely pierce the box top or bottom.
3. Cut the file cards in half. Number them 0 through 9, and again 0 through 9.

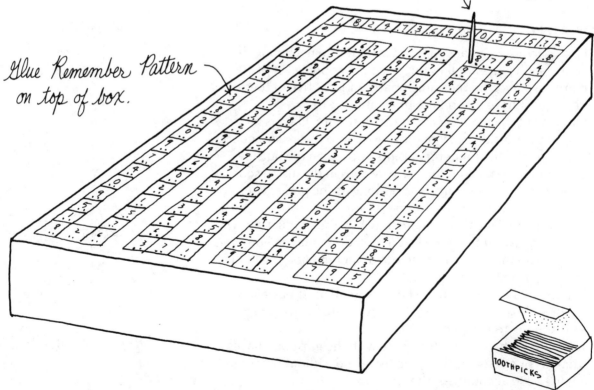

Punch holes with awl or nail.

Use toothpicks for markers.

Glue Remember Pattern on top of box.

HOW TO PLAY *(2 to 4 players)*

1. Place the toothpick markers at Start.
2. Thoroughly shuffle the deck of number cards at each turn, and place them facedown. The first player draws the top card from the deck. This card tells the player how many cards to draw.
3. The player puts the first card aside and then draws the indicated number of cards from the top of the deck.
4. The player may look at these cards three times by shuffling through them in the order they were drawn. The player then hands the cards to the other player (if there are two players) or to the person on the player's left (if there are three or four players).
5. The player then moves his or her marker through the sequence of numbers as the numbers appear on the game track. The correct move for the sequence 2-4-7-5 is shown in the illustration.
6. The player gets 1 point for each step on the board spanned by the sequence. If the player makes an error, the move ends at the last correct number in the sequence.
7. The players continue, in turn, until one wins with a score of 200 points.

■ **VARIATIONS**

1. Make new Remember games based on sequences of geometric figures, types of birds or trees, or names of places or people.
2. Base another Remember game on spelling skills. Put scrambled alphabets on the board and spelling stumpers on the draw cards. Players must go through the full sequence correctly or return to their previous position.

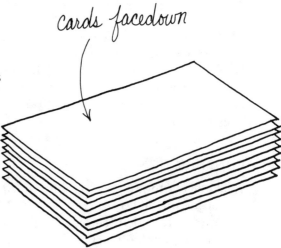

cards facedown

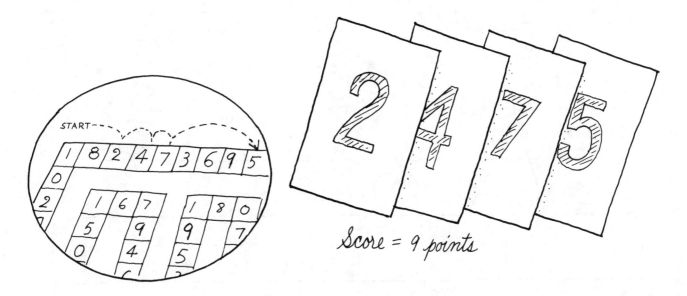

Score = 9 points

Change-Up

This game involves making multiple jumps and adding chains of numbers jumped. Since the rules may change as rapidly as the players move, this game demands concentration and imagination from everyone involved.

MATERIALS AND TOOLS

Box top or bottom
Change-Up Pattern (Game Sheet #11 on
  page 86)
Glue
Teetotum Spinner Pattern (Game Sheet #6 on
  page 81)
Scissors
Piece of cardboard 3 inches square
Dowel, 3/16 inch in diameter, 1 3/4 inches long
2 faucet washers
2 identical buttons for each player (to be used
  as markers)

CONSTRUCTION

1. Duplicate the Change-Up Pattern. Glue it thoroughly to the outside of the box.
2. Make a five-sided teetotum, using the Teetotum Spinner Pattern. Follow the directions given in the Spin Skittle Numbers game on page 22.

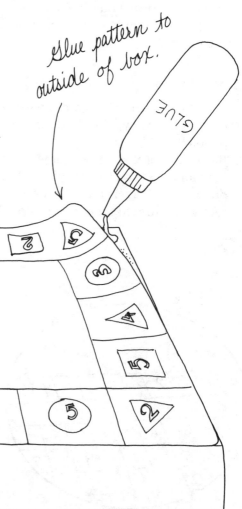

Glue pattern to outside of box.

HOW TO PLAY (2 or 3 players)

Place one marker outside square and one marker inside square.

1. Each player chooses any square as a starting point (but no two players may choose the same square). Each player puts one marker at the outside edge of the starting square and one marker inside the square. The first marker stays in place to mark the starting position while the second marker is moved.

2. Moves are made counterclockwise on the track. The triangle means move forward two spaces. The circle means move back one space. The square means stop, end of move.

3. The first player spins the teetotum, moves the indicated number of spaces, and continues jumping until he or she reaches a stop symbol. The number in each square that is touched is added to the player's score.

4. A player who lands in another player's starting square at any time during a move may then change the meaning of the symbols and the rules of the game. For example, the player may switch the meanings of the triangle, circle, and square, and/or change the movement from counterclockwise to clockwise.

5. A player who lands on his or her own starting square at any time during a move must stop there and miss a turn.

6. The players continue, in turn, until one wins with a total score of 100.

○ *This shape means move back 1 space.*

△ *This shape means move forward 2 spaces.*

□ *This shape means stop.*

■ VARIATION

Give double meanings to all steps in the game. The number indicated by the spin of the teetotum is counted both as score and the number of steps to be taken (for example, 3 points and three spaces). The diamond symbol means subtract and go forward two spaces. The circle means multiply and go back one space. The square means subtract and stop. Keep the other rules the same as in the original version.

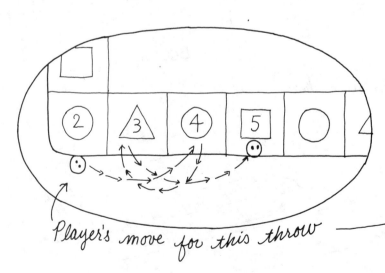

Player's move for this throw

Player's score = 12 points

Boxing Match

In this traditional game, players take turns selecting letters to fill out their secret grids with words and crosswords.

MATERIALS AND TOOLS

Box top or bottom
Boxing Match Pattern (Game Sheet #12 on page 87)
Letter Cards (Game Sheet #13 on page 88)
2 envelopes
4 paper clips
Glue
Scissors

CONSTRUCTION

1. Make two copies of the Boxing Match Pattern. Carefully fold each pattern along the dotted line so that the boxing-match side is folded forward onto the grid side.
2. Glue the top, blank halves of the surfaces together, back to back.
3. Glue the grid halves of the surfaces to the inside surface of the box top or bottom.
4. Link the paper clips together in two sets of two. These are used to hold up a screen between the two grids during play. (The screen is folded down when not in use.) Attach one paper clip from each set to a side of the box and the other paper clip to the screen. The illustration shows how the completed game should look.
5. Make two copies of the Letter Cards. Mount the copies on tagboard, cut each letter apart, and put the squares in a separate envelope.

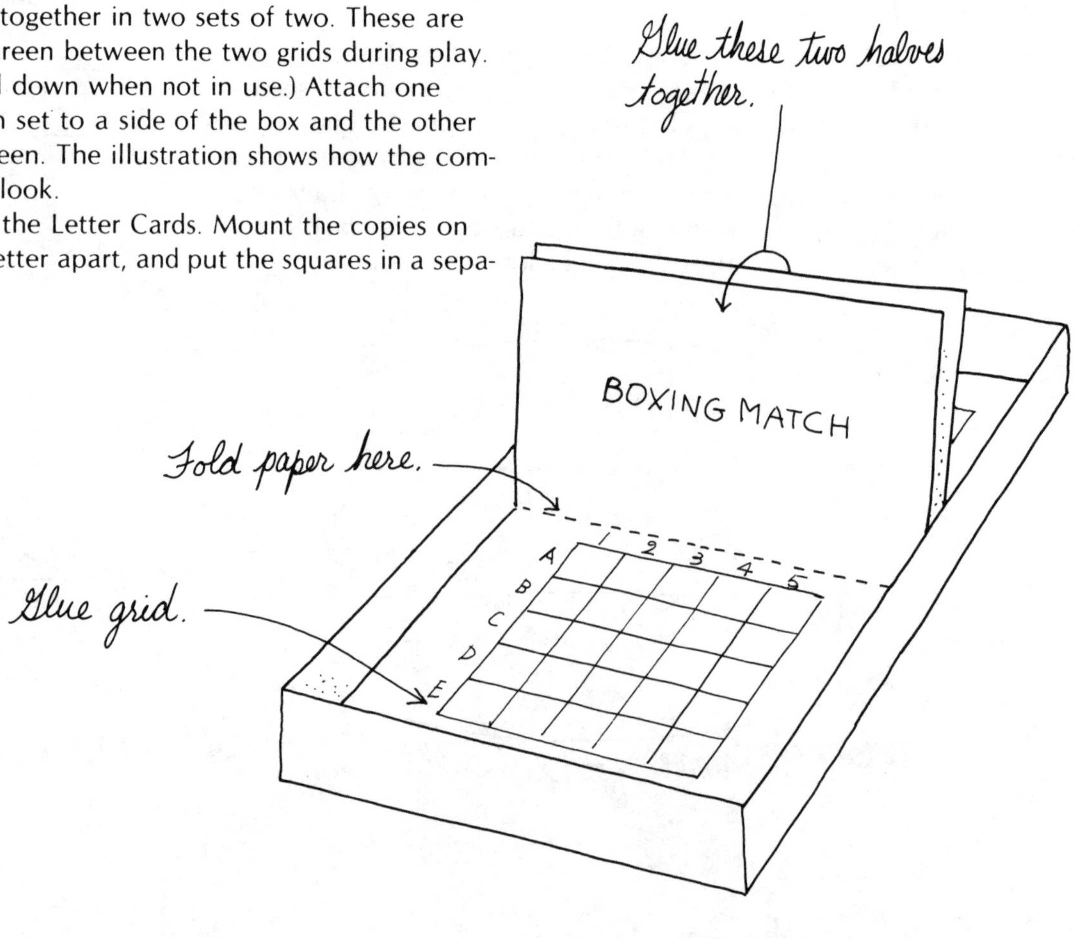

Glue these two halves together.

Fold paper here.

Glue grid.

BOXING MATCH

HOW TO PLAY *(2 players)*

1. Each player's goal is to form as many words as possible in the grid—from left to right (horizontally), from top to bottom (vertically), and from left to right moving up or down (diagonally). Players may not look at each other's grids.

2. The first player selects a letter from his or her alphabet envelope and plays it into any square in the grid. Once the letter has been played, it may not be moved.

3. The player calls out the letter. The second player must then place that letter into any square on his or her grid.

4. The second player then selects a letter, plays it, and calls it out. The first player must play the same letter into any square on his or her grid.

5. Players continue, in turn, until both their grids are filled with letters.

6. Players get 1 point for each letter in each word they have that has three letters or more. Only the longest word in each row, column, and diagonal counts. In the illustration, the player scores horizontally CART, ABLE, TOE, and HEART; vertically CATCH, ABOVE, LEG, TEAM, and BUT; and diagonally upward COLT. Total score for these words is 40 points.

■ VARIATIONS

1. Give points for words within words. Thus, both CAR and CART and both CAT and CATCH would score in the example shown. Also give points for words read right to left, bottom to top, or right to left diagonally. Under these rules, TUB and AGE (in the same example) would score.

2. Try Word Battleship. One player sets up a three-letter word, a four-letter word, and a five-letter word in the grid. The second player calls out the coordinates of squares on the grid (for example, A2, E5, or B1). The first player must say what letter, if any, is in the called square. This goes on until the second player gets or guesses all three words. Players then exchange roles and play again. The player who gets all three words in the fewest tries wins the game.

C	A	R	T	X
A	B	L	E	Z
T	O	E	A	B
C	V	G	M	U
H	E	A	R	T

Horizontally {
CART	4
ABLE	4
TOE	3
HEART	5

Vertically {
CATCH	5
ABOVE	5
LEG	3
TEAM	4
BUT	3

Diagonally { COLT   4

            40

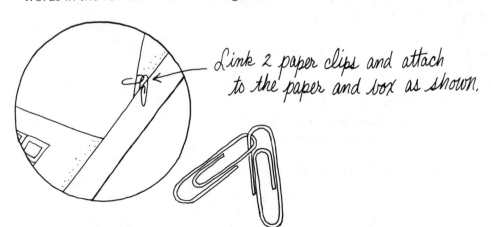

Link 2 paper clips and attach to the paper and box as shown.

Cover-Up

To succeed in this game players need good reading comprehension, logic, planning, and strategy. Being able to read and think clearly will help players cover and uncover the circles that will let them move forward.

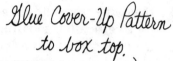

Glue Cover-Up Pattern to box top.

Cover circles 2, 4, 5, 6, and 8 with buttons.

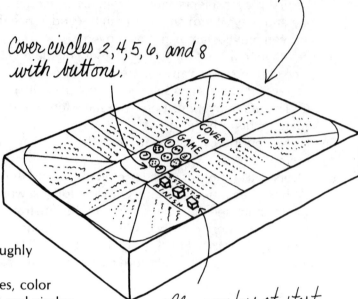

Place markers at start.

MATERIALS AND TOOLS

Box top or bottom
Cover-Up Pattern (Game Sheet #14 on page 89)
Glue
3 pencils or crayons: 1 red, 1 yellow, and 1 blue
5 small white shirt buttons
Marker for each player, each a different color
Penny

CONSTRUCTION

1. Duplicate the Cover-Up Pattern. Glue it thoroughly to the outside of the box top or bottom.
2. Without covering up the numerals in the circles, color circles 1, 3, and 8 blue, circles 2, 4, and 6 red, and circles 5, 7, and 9 yellow.

HOW TO PLAY *(2 to 4 players)*

1. Before the start of the game, place buttons to cover circles 2, 4, 5, 6, and 8.
2. Players place their markers at the Start position.
3. Each player takes a turn in three stages:
   A. The player may change the position of one button, but only in either of two ways: by moving the button in any direction into an adjoining open circle, or by jumping over another button into an open circle.
   B. The player then flips the penny to determine the first part of the move on the board. The player's marker is moved one space if the penny lands heads up, and two spaces if the penny lands tails up.
   C. The player completes the turn by following the directions in the space he or she lands in.
4. Other players may challenge any move if they suspect that a player has not followed directions properly. A player who fails to properly follow directions in a space must move back five spaces. A player who makes an incorrect challenge also must move back five spaces.
5. The first player to reach the Finish line is the winner.

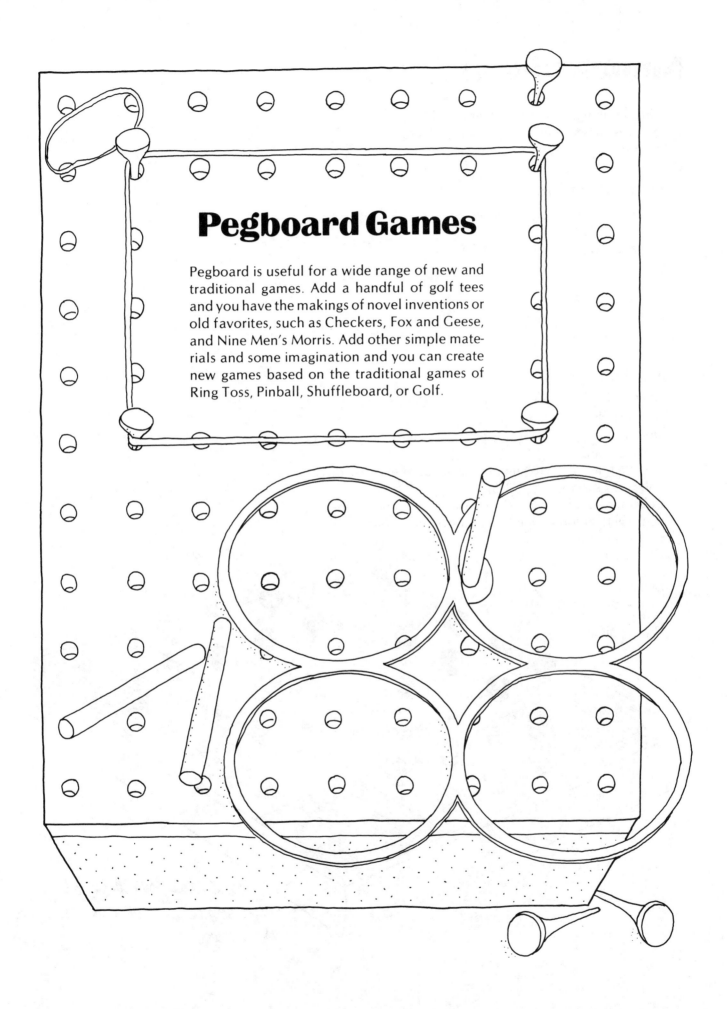

Pegboard Games

Pegboard is useful for a wide range of new and traditional games. Add a handful of golf tees and you have the makings of novel inventions or old favorites, such as Checkers, Fox and Geese, and Nine Men's Morris. Add other simple materials and some imagination and you can create new games based on the traditional games of Ring Toss, Pinball, Shuffleboard, or Golf.

Number Jump

Moving, jumping, and mixing their tees, players try to form lines that add up to an agreed-upon target number.

MATERIALS AND TOOLS

Pegboard, 7 inches square (7 holes by 7 holes)
Saw
Styrofoam, 1 inch thick and 7 inches square
Utility knife
Glue
Black felt-tip pen
24 golf tees, 12 each of 2 colors
Colored plastic tape

CONSTRUCTION

1. Cut the pegboard to size with the saw. Cut the Styrofoam to size with the utility knife.
2. Dot the Styrofoam with glue and attach it to the bottom of the pegboard.
3. Use the felt-tip pen to number the heads of each set of 12 golf tees as follows: 1, 2, 2, 3, 4, 5, 5, <u>6</u>, 7, 7, 8, <u>9</u>.
4. Cover the four holes (two by two) at each corner of the pegboard with colored tape so that the playing board looks like the illustration.

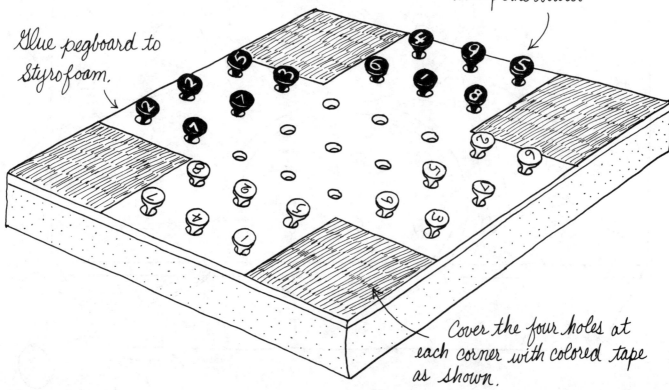

Glue pegboard to Styrofoam.

Example of one way to set up the board

Cover the four holes at each corner with colored tape as shown.

HOW TO PLAY (2 players)

1. Players decide on a target number between 12 and 20.
2. Each player sets up the other player's tees in any order. See the illustration for an example of how one board is set up at the beginning of a game.
3. Each player, in turn, moves one tee one space in any direction or jumps any one tee to enter an open space. The player may jump his or her own tee or the opponent's tee.
4. The object of a move is to form a line of tees, straight or diagonal, that adds up to the target number. The line can be made up of two, three, four, or more consecutive tees. There cannot be any gaps (empty holes) between the tees. The line can be made up of any combination of both players' tees.
5. A player earns 1 point for each move that makes the target number. In some cases, one move can produce the target number in two or more lines. Each line counts 1 point.
6. The first player to score 20 points wins.

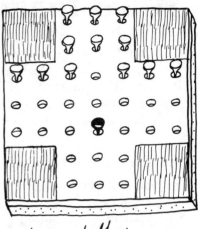

Fox and Geese

■ VARIATION

Play Fox and Geese, a game that's been played in many parts of the world for centuries. Set up 12 tees of one color (the geese) and one tee of another color (the fox), as shown in the illustration at the right.

The fox, who can move one space at a time in any direction, moves first. The fox may capture a goose (which is then removed from the board) by jumping over it and into an open space. The fox can also make double or triple jumps (as in the game of Checkers) if there are open spaces between the geese. If it can't move anywhere else, the fox must jump over a goose.

One goose at a time may move one space forward, sideways, or diagonally, but it cannot move back toward the starting position. Geese are not allowed to jump over the fox. The geese win if they can surround the fox or crowd it into a corner where it cannot move. The fox wins if it can get through the geese to the top of the board, where the geese cannot chase it, or if it captures so many geese that there aren't enough left to surround the fox.

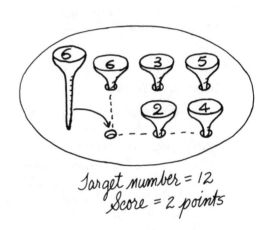

Target number = 12
Score = 2 points

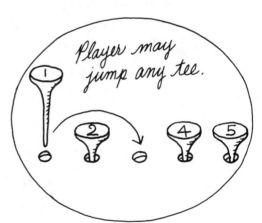

Player may jump any tee.

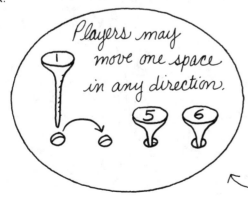

Players may move one space in any direction.

Target number = 12
Score = 1 point

Word Jump

This game challenges players' skills in vocabulary, spelling, and strategy, as well as their ability to make the most of chance. A teetotum spin tells how many jumps a player can make to find the needed letter for his or her word.

MATERIALS AND TOOLS

Pegboard, 7 inches square (7 holes by 7 holes)
Small saw
8 golf tees (4 to support the playing board, and 4 more—each of a different color—for the players' markers)
45 notebook hole reinforcements
Felt-tip pen
Teetotum Spinner Pattern (Game Sheet #6 on page 81)
Cardboard, 3 inches square
Dowel, 3/16 inch in diameter, 1 3/4 inches long
2 faucet washers
Glue

Pegboard

Paper hole reinforcements

Upside down tees in 4 corners

CONSTRUCTION

1. Cut the pegboard to size with the saw.
2. Insert a golf tee upside down in each of the four corner holes to support the board.
3. Place a notebook hole reinforcement over each of the 45 remaining holes in the board. Use the black felt-tip pen to mark them with the letters, as shown.
4. Make a five-sided teetotum. Duplicate the Teetotum Spinner Pattern. Cut out the five-sided teetotum pattern. Follow the directions in Spin Skittle Numbers on page 22 to complete the spinner. Mark the sides of the teetotum with the numbers 1 through 5.

Spin the teetotum to find out how many spaces to move the tee.

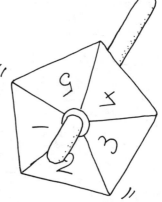

HOW TO PLAY *(2 to 4 players)*

1. Each player takes a playing tee of a different color. Each player assigns the starting point for the player on his or her right. No player can start in any one of the FREE holes or in the X hole.

2. The first player writes down the letter of his or her starting point, then spins the teetotum to find how many spaces to move the tee. Moves can be made forward, backward, to the right, or to the left, but not diagonally. The player can also change directions one or more times during a move.

3. The player writes down the letter of the hole in which the tee is placed at the end of the turn. If the tee ends up in one of the FREE holes, the player may write down any letter desired. If the tee ends up in the DOUBLE FREE hole, the player may write down any two letters desired, but must skip the next turn. A tee may not be moved into a hole already occupied by another tee, nor can it jump another tee.

4. Players try to reach letters that form a word in proper order. A letter that breaks the spelling order of a word may be crossed out, but it does not count in scoring. For example, a player may, in five turns, get the letters T E A B C H. That player may cross out the B, leaving the word TEACH.

5. In each of 10 turns, the player lists the letter reached. Each letter in a word counts 1 point, and a bonus point is added for each letter over four in a word. For example, JAB counts 3 points, TUBE counts 4, but QUART counts 6, and BIRTH-DAY counts 12.

6. The player with the most points at the end of the game is the winner.

■ VARIATION

Word Jump can be played as a solitaire game. The highest possible score is 16, for a 10-letter word made without the help of the DOUBLE FREE move. Can you do it?

TEABCH

Score = 6 points

Example of moves to make the word TEACH

Geo-Glob

The Earthlings' player in this game must contend with the changing area and angles of the ferocious Glob. Can at least one Earthling escape the Glob's sprawling geometry? Play and find out!

MATERIALS AND TOOLS

Pegboard, 7 inches wide and 12 inches long (7 holes by 12 holes)
Small saw
Styrofoam, 1 inch thick, 7 inches wide, and 12 inches long
Utility knife
Glue
Teetotum Spinner Pattern (Game Sheet #6 on page 81)
Scissors
Black felt-tip pen
Dowel, 3/16 inch in diameter, 1 3/4 inches long
2 faucet washers
8 golf tees
Rubber band, about 6 inches in circumference
Cardboard, 3 inches square

CONSTRUCTION

1. Cut the pegboard to size with the saw. Cut the Styrofoam to size with the utility knife.
2. Dot the Styrofoam with glue and attach it firmly to the back of the pegboard.
3. Duplicate the Teetotum Spinner Pattern. Cut out the five-sided teetotum. Trace it onto the cardboard and cut along the edges. Mark it as shown in the illustration. Complete the teetotum according to the directions given in the Spin Skittle Game on page 22.
4. Make the Glob by looping the rubber band around three golf tees.

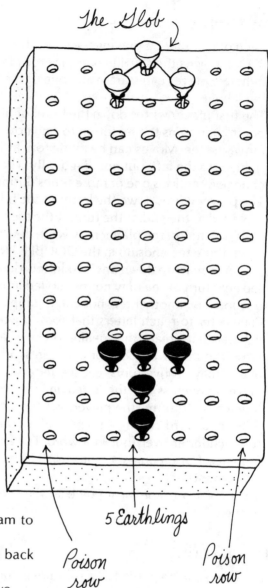

The Glob

5 Earthlings

Poison row

Poison row

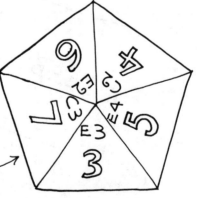

Mark teetotum as shown.

HOW TO PLAY *(2 players)*

1. Set up the Geo-Glob Game as shown in the illustration.
2. The Earthlings' player takes the first turn, spinning the teetotum to find out the number of spaces to move. The Earthlings' player uses the outside numbers on the teetotum; the Glob uses the inside numbers. The five Earthling pieces can move in any direction—forward, backward, sideways, or diagonally. The number that shows on the teetotum can be used to move one or more pieces. For example, if the teetotum shows 3, the player can move one piece three spaces, three pieces one space each, or one piece two spaces and another piece one space. The rows at the far right and left are poisonous to Earthlings and cannot be used by them. A piece placed in either one of these rows instantly "dies," and must be removed from the game.
3. The Glob player takes the second turn, spinning the teetotum to find out the number of spaces to move. The teetotum shows both Expand (E2, E3, and E4) and Contract (C2, C3) directions for the Glob. If an Expand number comes up, the Glob can grow outward by that many spaces. The Glob's parts can move outward only in a straight line forward, back, or sideways; they cannot move diagonally. If a Contract number comes up, the Glob's parts must be moved inward as many spaces as possible, up to the number shown. The number that shows on the teetotum can be used to move one or more parts of the Glob. For example, if the teetotum shows E3, one part of the Glob can be moved three spaces, or three parts of the Glob can be moved one space each. Since the Glob is not affected by the poison rows, its parts can be moved into these rows.
4. If any Earthling falls completely inside the Glob, it is captured and removed from the game. However, if an Earthling falls inside the Glob but is still touched by one of its sides, it may escape.
5. The Earthlings win the game if any one of them survives and reaches the end of the board opposite their starting point. The Glob wins the game if it captures all the Earthlings before they reach the end of the board.

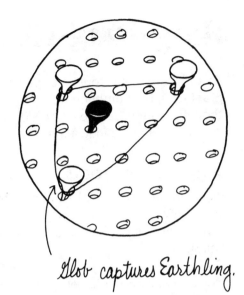

Glob captures Earthling.

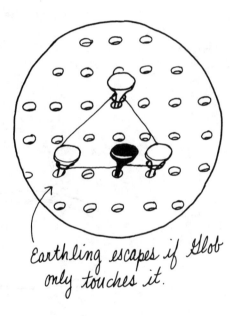

Earthling escapes if Glob only touches it.

Loop rubber band around golf tees this way.

Ring-Ring-Ring-Ring Toss

An old game times four gives players lots of practice in big-number multiplication. Although a winning score of 20,000 sounds high, it can be achieved in just a few tosses.

MATERIALS AND TOOLS

Pegboard, 5 inches square (5 holes by 5 holes)
Small saw
Styrofoam, 1 inch thick and 5 inches square
Utility knife
Glue
Dowel, $3/16$ inch in diameter and 16 inches long
Sandpaper
4 notebook hole reinforcements
Felt-tip pen
3 plastic frames from 3 canned beverage six-packs
Scissors

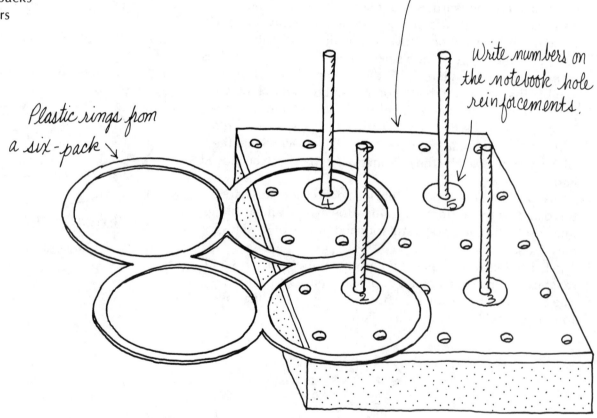

Pegboard glued to Styrofoam

Write numbers on the notebook hole reinforcements.

Plastic rings from a six-pack

Score: 2 × 4 = 8

CONSTRUCTION

1. Cut the pegboard to size with the saw. Cut the Styrofoam to size with the utility knife.
2. Dot the Styrofoam with glue and attach it firmly to the back of the pegboard.
3. Saw the doweling into four 4-inch pieces. Sandpaper one end of each piece so that the pieces can be pushed easily through the holes in the pegboard.
4. Place the notebook hole reinforcements around the holes that are one space diagonally inward from the corners of the pegboard. Mark the reinforcements with the scoring values of 2, 3, 4, and 5. Then push the pieces of dowel into these holes. The finished target board is shown in the illustration.
5. Cut away the two end rings from each of the plastic six-pack frames, leaving three four-ring frames.

Discard this pair of rings.

HOW TO PLAY (2 to 4 players)

1. The target board is placed on a tabletop. Each player, in turn, throws the three plastic frames at the board from a sitting or standing position three feet away.
2. A player scores for each peg encircled by a ring in the frames (however, there is no score for a peg encircled by the opening between the rings in the frame). All scoring values are multiplied by each other. The first player to reach a total of 20,000 is the winner. Note that this score is a reasonable goal for a good player. One perfect throw—four pegs ringed— scores $2 \times 3 \times 4 \times 5$, or 120; two perfect throws score 120 $\times$ 120, or 14,400, and three perfect throws score 1,728,000!

■ VARIATIONS

1. Play by all the rules above, but also divide the total score by the value of any peg circled by the opening between the rings in the plastic frame.
2. Play G-O-A-T, a nonsense form of Ring Toss. One player throws, ringing one, two, three, or four of the pegs. The next player throws, attempting to ring the same number of pegs as the first player. If the second player fails to match the first, he or she is given the G in GOAT. The second player then goes first, and the other player tries to match the throw. The game proceeds in this fashion until one player has collected all four letters, thus becoming the GOAT.

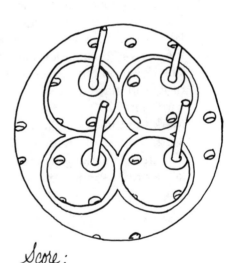

Score:
$2 \times 3 \times 4 \times 5 = 120$ points

Word Golf

In this game, skill or luck may enable players to win the key word with a hole-in-one shot. But even if they take more strokes, they can still make points by finding words within the key words.

MATERIALS AND TOOLS

Pegboard, 7 inches wide and 14 inches long (7 holes by 14 holes)
Small saw
Corrugated cardboard, 2 inches wide and 11½ inches long
Scissors
Masking tape, 1 inch wide and 8 feet long
3 notebook hole reinforcements
Felt-tip pen
Flat-edged toothpick
Round bead or ball bearing, ³/₁₆ inch in diameter
File cards (for keeping score)

CONSTRUCTION

1. Cut the pegboard to size with the saw.
2. Cut the cardboard into ½-inch strips.
3. Follow the diagram to build the Word Golf course. To make the fairway boundaries, place a strip of masking tape sticky-side down on the pegboard, lay a strip of cardboard on top of it, and place another strip of masking tape on top of the cardboard.
4. Mark the three holes with the notebook reinforcements.
5. Mark the tee-off areas, as shown in the diagram, with a single strip of masking tape. Use the felt-tip pen to write in the key words, as indicated.

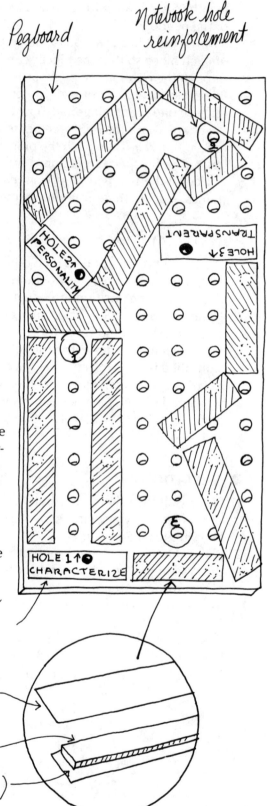

Pegboard

Notebook hole reinforcement

HOLE 2↑ PERSONALITY

TRANSPARENT
HOLE 3↑

HOLE 1↑ CHARACTERIZE

Write on the masking tape with a felt-tip pen.

Masking tape (sticky-side down)

Cardboard

Masking tape (sticky-side down)

HOW TO PLAY *(2 to 4 players)*

1. The first player places the ball (the bead or ball bearing) in the tee-off area for hole 1 and strikes it toward the hole with the broad end of the toothpick. If the ball goes into the hole with one stroke, the player wins the key word *characterize* for the hole. If the player takes two or more strokes to get the ball in the hole, one letter must be taken away from the key word for each stroke, and the longest word the player can think of must be formed from the remaining letters. For example, a player who takes three strokes to get into the hole removes the letters *i, z,* and *e,* ending up with the word *character.* Players who take more strokes should be able to form such words as *charter, teach, chart, act,* or others. Players may not form a word already made by a player before them, but they may rearrange the remaining letters. Use the file cards to form words and keep score.

2. Each player, in turn, plays the first hole and counts the number of letters in the word to get a score. The player who gets the shortest word on the first hole plays first on the second hole; the player with the longest word on the first hole plays last on the second hole.

3. The game continues in this manner through all three holes. The winner is the player with the greatest total number of letters in the words won.

4. Replace the tee-off strips after each game, inserting new key words. Key words should, of course, be long words that offer many possibilities for forming words within words.

■ **VARIATION**

Use a larger piece of pegboard to build a nine-hole Word Golf course. Indicate the key word for the first hole only. After that, let the winner of each hole provide the key word for the following hole.

Keep score this way. →

Hole 1 : 3 strokes   Donna's score

CHARACTER~~IZE~~ = CHARACTER   9 points

Hole 2 : 5 strokes
PERSON~~ALITY~~ = PERSON   6 points

Hole 3 : 6 strokes
~~TRANSPARENT~~ = SPARE   5 points

                                     20 points

Pinball Math

The bounding marbles set up a chain reaction that the player must calculate instantly to get a score. Players may rearrange the game for greater action or challenge.

MATERIALS AND TOOLS

Pegboard, 14 inches square (14 holes by 14 holes)
Board or plywood, 1 inch thick, 3 inches wide, and 14 inches long
Small saw
4 nails or screws
Hammer or screwdriver
Strip of corrugated cardboard, 2 inches wide and 14 inches long
Scissors or utility knife
Glue
36 golf tees (white, yellow, or another light color)
Felt-tip pen
14 thin rubber bands, 6 to 8 inches in circumference
5 marbles, about ½ inch in diameter

CONSTRUCTION

1. Cut the pegboard and the wood to size with the saw.
2. Attach the wood to one end of the pegboard with the nails or screws.
3. Cut out the corrugated cardboard with a scissors or utility knife, and mark it according to the diagram.
4. Dot the cardboard piece with glue and attach it to the lower end of the pegboard, opposite the elevated end.
5. Mark the heads of the golf tees with the felt-tip pen and place the tees in the pegboard in the pattern, as shown.
6. Double up (or redouble up, if necessary) the rubber bands, and stretch them tightly between the tees, as shown. Loop some of them straight around the tees, and twist others in the middle to make a figure eight.

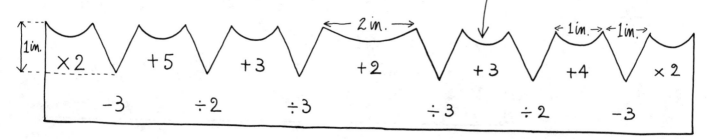

Mark cardboard with felt-tip pen.

HOW TO PLAY (2 to 4 players)

1. The first player places each marble on top of one of the tees marked X at the top of the board, then flicks it into play with a finger. The player plays all five marbles in succession. Any marble that falls off the board may be played again.

2. When all five marbles have fallen into one of the pockets on the board or dropped to the bottom, the player must quickly work the chain calculation of all score values by going from left to right and top to bottom. For example, the chain calculation for the illustration is: $4 \times 2 + 10 \div 3 + 3 = 9$.

3. Players may, by agreement, change the position of any of the pockets or the individual tees at any time during the game.

4. Players continue in turn until one wins with a total score of 50.

◼ VARIATION

Play Jet Pinball Math. Each player, in turn, uses just one marble. A score is counted for each pocket that the marble touches until it comes to a stop. The score must be calculated as the marble moves around the board.

The score of this game is $4 \times 2 + 10 \div 3 + 3 = 9$

Attach wood to pegboard with screws.

Glue cardboard to pegboard.

Pegboard Concentration

This game requires players to match synonyms. The game can also be adapted to many other kinds of subject matter, offering a wide range of possibilities for the development of language skills.

MATERIALS AND TOOLS

Pegboard, 6 inches square (6 holes by 6 holes)
Small saw
4 1-inch cubes of wood or Styrofoam
Glue
32 2-inch squares of paper
Felt-tip pen
Finish nail, 3 inches long

CONSTRUCTION

1. Cut the pegboard to size with the saw.
2. Glue a wood or Styrofoam cube underneath the pegboard at each of the four corners.
3. Make 32 paper pegs out of the squares of paper. Before it is assembled into a peg, mark each piece of paper with one synonym from the list at the right.
4. To make a paper peg, lay the square with the word face-down. Starting on the side of the square opposite the word, roll the paper tightly onto a finish nail. When you have rolled to within 1/2 inch of the edge, apply glue to the portion not yet rolled onto the nail. Complete the rolling, then pull out the nail.

HOW TO PLAY (2 to 4 players)

1. Players quickly put the pegs, marked ends down, into the pegboard holes without studying the words on the pegs.
2. The first player pulls two pegs from their holes and reads the words on them. If the words are synonymous with each other, the player keeps them and continues the turn. If the words are not synonymous with each other, the player returns them to their holes, meanwhile trying to memorize their positions for possible future matches. All players should observe one another's moves.
3. Players continue in turn until all synonyms have been matched and all pegs have been removed from the board. The player with the most pegs at the end of the game is the winner.

Glue Styrofoam to pegboard.

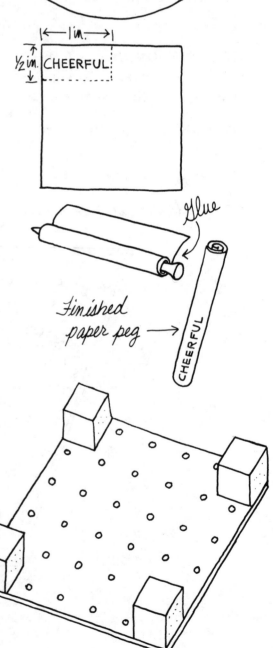

happy, glad, cheerful, elated
sad, downcast, gloomy, depressed
angry, irate, furious, irritated
intelligent, brainy, learned, smart
strong, powerful, muscular, brawny
small, little, diminutive, tiny
quiet, silent, still, hushed
tired, weary, sleepy, fatigued

CHEERFUL

Glue

Finished paper peg →

CHEERFUL

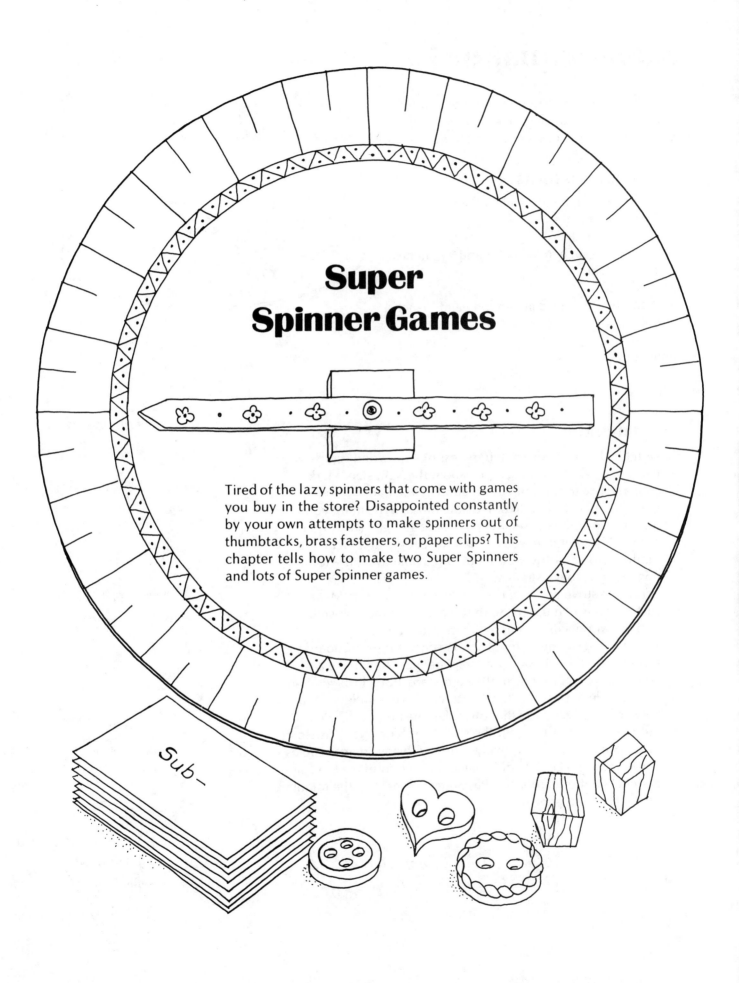

Super Spinner Games

Tired of the lazy spinners that come with games you buy in the store? Disappointed constantly by your own attempts to make spinners out of thumbtacks, brass fasteners, or paper clips? This chapter tells how to make two Super Spinners and lots of Super Spinner games.

Sub_

Super Spinner I

If finding and using a drill are no problem for you, then go for Super Spinner I. It's sturdy, very efficient, and costs next to nothing.

MATERIALS AND TOOLS

Scrap of 1-inch pine or ³/₄-inch plywood, about 2¹/₂ inches square
Drill with ⁵/₃₂-inch drill bit
Stove bolt, ⁵/₃₂ inch in diameter and 1¹/₂ inches long, with nut
Screwdriver
Stiff cardboard strip, 8 inches long and ³/₄ inch wide
Scissors
Paper punch
Faucet washer, rubber or plastic
Glue

CONSTRUCTION

1. Don't be fussy about the squareness of your wood scrap—it can be any shape as long as it's about the right size. Mark a spot as close to the center of the top as you can.
2. Use a ⁵/₃₂-inch drill bit to drill a hole through the mark you have made at the center. Keep the hole straight. (If a drill is not readily available, you can ask the people at a local lumberyard or hardware store to drill a hole for you—for a nominal fee, they usually will.)
3. Screw the stove bolt into the hole from the bottom. Make sure to screw it in tightly, so that the head of the bolt sinks into the wood. Put the nut on tightly from the top.
4. To make the spinner arrow, trim one end of the cardboard to a point with the scissors. Use the paper punch to make a hole in the exact middle of the cardboard. Put a little glue on the flat side of the washer, and attach it to the underside of the cardboard arrow so that the holes line up.
5. Put the spinner arrow onto the stove-bolt base. Now just spin away! Super Spinner I is ready to use with any spinner circles you want to make. Use the Spinner Pattern to make the spinner circle out of cardboard. Put Super Spinner I in the middle of the circle, as shown.

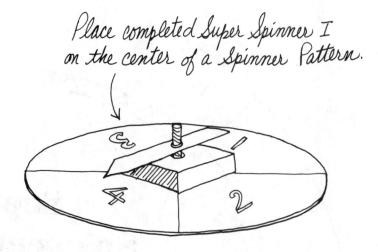

Place completed Super Spinner I on the center of a Spinner Pattern.

Screw nut on bolt from the top.

Screw stove bolt in hole from the bottom.

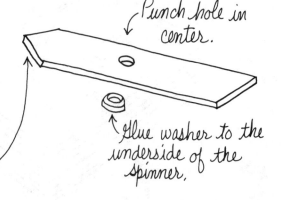

Punch hole in center.

Glue washer to the underside of the spinner.

Trim cardboard to a point.

Super Spinner II

If you don't want to use a drill or you have a problem finding one, Super Spinner II is the next best spinner to make.

MATERIALS AND TOOLS

2 pieces of pegboard, each 3 inches square (3 holes by 3 holes)
Stove bolt, $5/32$ inch in diameter and $1\frac{1}{2}$ inches long
4 stove bolts, each $5/32$ inch in diameter and $3/4$ inch long
10 nuts (2 for each bolt)
Stiff cardboard strip, $3/4$ inch wide and 8 inches long
Scissors
Paper punch
Faucet washer, rubber or plastic
Glue

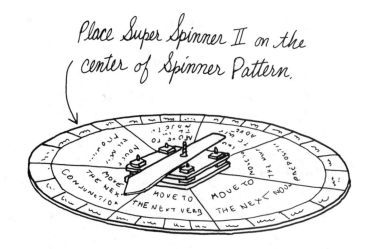

Place Super Spinner II on the center of Spinner Pattern.

CONSTRUCTION

1. From the bottom, push the longer bolt through the center hole of one of the pieces of pegboard. Fasten the nut tightly on top.
2. From the bottom, push the four shorter bolts through the four corner holes of the pegboard. Fasten the nuts tightly on top.
3. Put the second piece of pegboard over the bolts. Fasten the remaining five nuts over the five bolts, as shown. This base is now ready for use with the spinner arrow, as described in steps 4 and 5 of Super Spinner I.

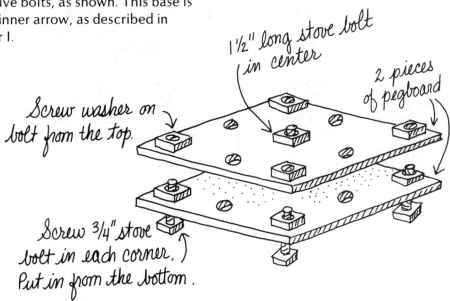

Screw washer on bolt from the top.

$1\frac{1}{2}$" long stove bolt in center

2 pieces of pegboard

Screw $3/4$" stove bolt in each corner. Put in from the bottom.

Parts of Speech Spin

Here is a spinner game and a board game all in one. Players move to the next word on the track that represents the part of speech shown on the spinner. What's unusual about this game is that players try to come in second, rather than first, place.

MATERIALS AND TOOLS

Super Spinner
Parts of Speech Circle (Game Sheet #16 on page 92)
2 small buttons or other markers, each a different color
Scissors

CONSTRUCTION

1. Duplicate the Parts of Speech Circle.
2. Place the Super Spinner in the center of the circle.

HOW TO PLAY *(2 players)*

1. Players place their markers at the Start position in the track on the outer edge of the circle.
2. Each player, in turn, spins and moves to the first example of the part of speech indicated by the spinner.
3. If the second player challenges, the first player must use the word in a sentence to show that it can be used as the part of speech in question. For instance, a player may move to *bow* as the next verb in the track. The second player may challenge, saying that *bow* is a noun. The first player must then use *bow* as a verb in a sentence, such as: "The man refused to *bow* his head."
4. The first player to reach the word *END* loses the game. Note that *END* must be played as a noun, a verb, or an adjective. A player does not have to make the final move to this space unless one of these three parts of speech comes up on the spinner.

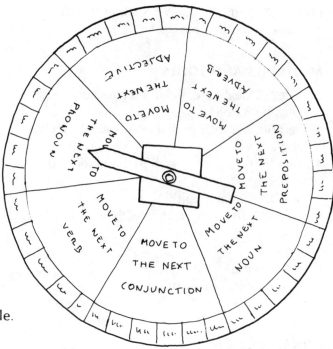

Use buttons as markers.

Making Dozens

Three Super Spinners are needed to turn out the numbers that players try to make into any multiple of 12. Players use addition and subtraction in the attempt to reach even dozens.

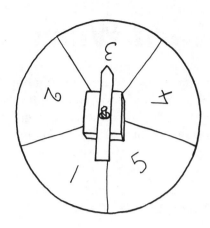

MATERIALS AND TOOLS

Spinner Pattern (Game Sheet #15 on page 91)
Scissors
3 sheets of paper, 8½ inches wide and 11 inches long
Felt-tip pens in 3 different colors
3 Super Spinners

CONSTRUCTION

1. Duplicate the Spinner Pattern. Trace and cut out three spinner circles, each divided into five segments.
2. Use the felt-tip pens to mark each spinner circle with the numerals 1 through 5. Use the three colors so that the like numerals are a different color on each spinner. For example, make the 1 red on the first spinner circle, blue on the second spinner circle, and green on the third spinner circle.

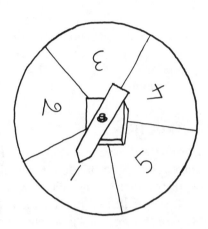

HOW TO PLAY (2 to 4 players)

1. Each player, in turn, spins all three spinners. The three numbers that come up may be added or subtracted in any sequence to make the player's count for the round. For example, 1, 3, and 5 may be calculated as $1 + 3 + 5 = 9$, or $(3 - 1) + 5 = 7$, or $(5 - 3) + 1 = 3$, or $5 - (3 + 1) = 1$.
2. Players try to accumulate a count that is an exact multiple of 12, except for 12×1. The count for each turn is added to, or subtracted from, the accumulated count for all previous turns.
3. A player who spins three like numerals, such as 1, 1, 1 or 5, 5, 5, or spins three unlike numerals of the same color may take an extra turn.
4. A round ends when a player reaches any count that is an exact multiple of 12: 36, 60, 84, 108, 132, and so on.
5. The winner of a round scores 12 points. The first player to score 36 points wins the game.

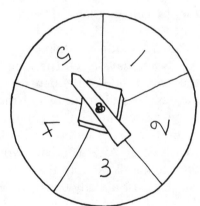

These 3 spins can be counted

$$1 + 3 + 5 = 9$$
or
$$(3 - 1) + 5 = 7$$
or
$$(5 - 3) + 1 = 3$$
or
$$5 - (3 + 1) = 1$$

Word Whirl

This game uses four Super Spinners to give players a chance to make small words into bigger ones, both common and uncommon. Although the game is self-checking, it can be used as a starter for vocabulary-building work with the dictionary, too.

MATERIALS AND TOOLS

Spinner Pattern (Game Sheet #15 on page 91)
Scissors
4 sheets of paper, 8½ inches wide and 11 inches long
Felt-tip pens in 4 different colors
4 Super Spinners

CONSTRUCTION

1. Duplicate the Spinner Pattern. Trace and cut out four spinner circles, each divided into eight segments.
2. Mark the first spinner circle with the following letters, one in each segment: B C D F G H L T. Mark the second spinner circle with the following letters, one in each segment: M N P R S T W B. Mark two letters in the first color, two in the second color, two in the third color, and two in the fourth color.
3. The third and fourth spinners are marked with three-letter words and have a self-checking list of expanded words on the reverse side of the paper under each of the words (see page 55). Again, mark two of the words on the top of each spinner circle in the first color, two words in the second color, two words in the third color, and two words in the fourth color. After you have written each word on top of the spinner circle, turn the circle over and write the self-checking list directly under the word, as shown.

write every 2 letters in a different color. Four colors to a wheel.

write every 2 words in a different color

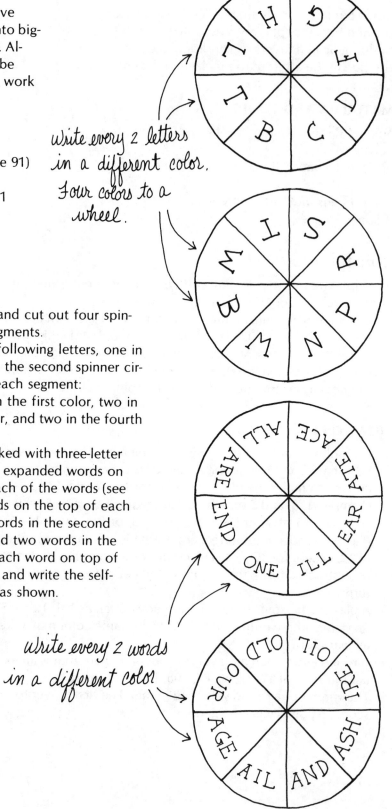

Word	Self-Checking List
one	bone, cone, done, gone, hone, long, none, pone, tone
ill	bill, dill, fill, gill, hill, mill, pill, rill, sill, till, will
ear	bear, dear, fear, gear, hear, near, pear, rear, sear, tear, wear
ate	bate, date, fate, gate, hate, late, mate, pate, rate, sate
ace	dace, face, lace, mace, pace, race
all	ball, call, fall, gall, hall, mall, pall, tall, wall
are	bare, care, dare, fare, hare, mare, pare, rare, tare
end	bend, fend, lend, mend, rend, send, tend, wend

These are the words and the self-checking list for the third spinner circle.

Word	Self-Checking List
ail	bail, fail, hail, mail, nail, pail, rail, sail, tail, wail
and	band, hand, land, sand, wand
ash	bash, cash, dash, gash, hash, lash, mash, rash, sash, wash
ire	dire, fire, hire, mire, sire, tire, wire
oil	boil, coil, foil, moil, roil, toil
old	bold, cold, fold, gold, hold, mold, sold, told
our	dour, four, hour, pour, sour, tour
age	cage, gage, page, rage, sage, wage

These are for the fourth spinner circle.

HOW TO PLAY *(2 to 6 players)*

1. Each player, in turn, spins all four spinners, then tries to make new words by adding the single letters on the first two spinner circles to the fronts of the three-letter words on the second two spinner circles.
2. Players score 1 point for each word made. Players should be able to score from 1 to 4 points per turn. A player can make 4 points, for example, by spinning *p* and *f* and *ail* and *ear*, and identifying the words *pail, pear, fail,* and *fear*.
3. A player who spins items of the same color on all four spinners gets an extra turn.
4. Players may challenge another player's word. To settle the challenge, players lift the edge of the spinner circle and consult the self-checking list. (If the word on the self-checking list is in dispute, or if it does not appear on the list, players may consult a dictionary.) The player who identifies a nonword loses the next turn. If the challenged word is on the self-checking list, the player gets an extra turn.
5. Players continue, in turn, until one wins the game with a score of 25 points.

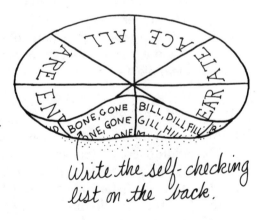

Write the self-checking list on the back.

Threat from Outer Space

A Terror Ship from outer space is heading toward Earth on a direct course. The two captains, of Starship I and Starship II, have the mission of cutting off or destroying the Terror Ship. Two Super Spinners give the coordinates that either captain must choose to fight the invader most effectively.

MATERIALS AND TOOLS

Spinner Pattern (Game Sheet #15 on page 91)
Scissors
2 sheets of paper, 8¹/₂ inches wide and 11 inches long
4 felt-tip pens, 1 black and 3 other colors
Graph paper, 5¹/₂ inches square (4 squares to the inch)
2 Super Spinners

CONSTRUCTION

1. Duplicate the Spinner Pattern. Trace and cut out two spinner circles, each divided into eight segments.
2. Mark one spinner circle with the numbers 1 through 8, one number to a segment. Mark the other spinner circle with the letters A through H, one letter to a segment. Use the black felt-tip pen to mark two of the items on each spinner circle, and the other three colors to mark another two items each on each spinner circle.
3. Copy the diagram on the square of graph paper. (For repeat games, either make duplicate copies or cover the diagram with clear plastic so that marks can be erased.)

HOW TO PLAY (2 players)

1. At the start of the game, the Terror Ship moves to coordinate A8. Its future course (one move per turn) will take it to B7, C6, D5, E4, F3, G2, H1, and then to Earth.
2. The captains of Starship I and Starship II must stop the Terror Ship. They can do this by cutting across its course (always in front of the Terror Ship) three times, or by reaching the exact coordinate occupied by the Terror Ship. The players spin both Super Spinners, giving the coordinate to which one of the two Starships may move. Only one of the Starships can move each turn; the captains decide which one it will be. The moves of each Starship are marked in a different color.

3. If the colors of the number and the letter on the spinner circles match, the captains get an extra turn. If the number and the letter spun are both black, the captains lose their next turn.
4. As the game continues, the Terror Ship makes one move (along the path marked by a black line), and the Starship captains spin for their moves. If the Starships manage to cross three times in front of the Terror Ship, or if one of the Starships lands directly on the coordinate where the Terror Ship is located, the game ends and Earth is saved. If the Starships cannot stop the Terror Ship before it passes H1, Earth is lost.

■ VARIATION

Players can devise an expanded version of the game, using co-ordinates 1–20 and A–T, by plotting different, less direct courses for three Terror Ships. Can the two Starships foil the threat to Earth this time?

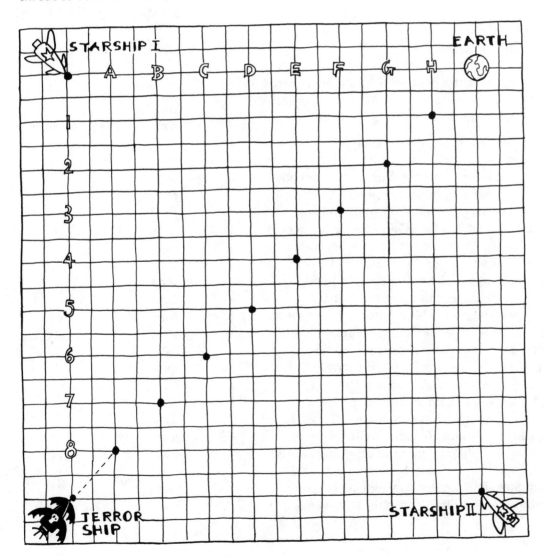

Roots and Offshoots

The Super Spinner points out Latin roots, and players find how many words they can make by adding the prefixes found on their playing cards.

MATERIALS AND TOOLS

Spinner Pattern (Game Sheet #15 on page 91)
Scissors
2 sheets of paper, 8½ inches wide and 11
   inches long
Felt-tip pen
13 file cards or slips of paper, 5 inches wide and
   3 inches long
Super Spinner

CONSTRUCTION

1. Duplicate the Spinner Pattern. Trace and cut out a spinner circle divided into 20 segments.
2. Write the roots shown at the right on each segment.
3. Write the prefixes shown at the right on the 13 playing cards.
4. Copy the following self-checking list of words onto a sheet of paper 8½ inches wide and 11 inches long:

Accede, Access, Addict, Adduce, Admit, Advent, Adverse, Advise, Append, Appose, Ascribe, Aspect, Aspire, Assist, Attain, Attend, Attract, Avert, Commit, Compose, Concede, Conduce, Conduct, Confer, Congress, Conscribe, Conscript, Consist, Conspire, Contain, Contend, Contract, Convent, Converse, Convert, Deduce, Deduct, Defer, Depend, Deport, Depose, Describe, Desist, Detain, Detract, Devise, Edict, Egress, Eject, Emit, Exceed, Excess, Exist, Expect, Expend, Expire, Export, Expose, Extend, Extract, Event, Impend, Import, Impose, Indict, Induce, Infer, Ingress, Inject, Inscribe, Insist, Inspect, Inspire, Intend, Intercede, Interject, Interpose, Invent, Inverse, Invert, Object, Obtain, Obverse, Offer, Omit, Oppose, Permit, Persist, Perspire, Pertain, Perverse, Pervert, Precede, Predict, Prefer, Prescribe, Pretend, Prevent, Proceed, Process, Produce, Product, Progress, Project, Propose, Proscribe, Prospect, Protract, Recede, Recess, Reduce, Refer, Regress, Reject, Remit, Report, Repose, Resist, Respect, Respire, Retain, Retract, Reverse, Revert, Revise, Subject, Submit, Subscribe, Subsist, Subtract, Subvert, Succeed, Success, Suffer, Support, Suppose, Suspect, Sustain, Transfer, Transgress, Transmit, Transport, Transpose, Transcribe, Transpire, Transverse.

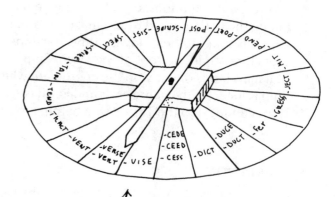

Write roots on each segment of the circle.

-cede ⎫
-ceed ⎬ *(all three in one segment)*
-cess ⎭
-dict
-duce ⎫
-duct ⎬ *(both in one segment)*
-fer
-gress
-ject
-mit
-pend
-port
-pose
-scribe
-sist
-spect
-spire
-tain
-tend
-tract
-vent
-verse ⎫
-vert ⎬ *(both in one segment)*
-vise

HOW TO PLAY *(2 to 4 players)*

1. Shuffle the 13 prefix cards and place them facedown. Each player draws one card.

2. Any player can spin the spinner. All players look at the root indicated by the spinner and, if possible, combine it with the prefixes on their cards to form words. Players may make only one word with their own prefix card.

3. Players write down their words and announce them. If any player is challenged, he or she consults the self-checking list. However, there is no penalty for a nonword, except that the player must cross it out.

4. Each word made counts 1 point. After each turn is completed, the player (or players, if there is a tie) with the lowest accumulated total score is allowed to draw an extra prefix card and try to make a word. The players then return all the prefix cards to the bottom of the pile and draw again from the top.

5. The game continues until one player wins with a score of 10 points.

■ **VARIATION**

Players are allowed to make 1 point or 1 bonus point by adding a suffix other than *-ing* or *-ed* to their words. Examples of words formed in this manner are *Pro-cess-ion, Ad-ject-ive, Pro-pos-al, In-spect-or,* and *At-tain-ment.*

Ad-	*(can change to A-, Ac-, Ap-, As-, or At-)*
Com-	*(can change to Con-)*
De-	
Ex-	*(can change to E-. Also, drop the s from roots that begin with s.)*
In-	*(can change to Im-)*
Inter-	
Ob-	*(can change to O-, Of-, or Op-)*
Per-	
Pre-	
Pro-	
Re-	
Sub-	*(can change to Su-, Suc-, Suf-, Sup-, or Sus-)*
Trans-	

Write prefixes on 13 playing cards.

Going for Distance

The biggest U.S. cities are shown on two Super Spinners. Players spin to find the two cities between which they will travel, piling up the mileage to take them the 20,000 miles around the outside spinner track.

MATERIALS AND TOOLS

Spinner Pattern (Game Sheet #15 on page 91)
Scissors
2 pieces of paper, 8½ inches wide and 11 inches long, or larger
Compass
Felt-tip pens of various colors
2 Super Spinners
2 small buttons or other markers

CONSTRUCTION

1. Duplicate the Spinner Pattern.
2. Make two spinner circles 7 inches in diameter, or larger.
3. Use a compass to make a circle about ½ inch from the edge of the larger circles.
4. Using the Spinner Pattern, divide the outer track of each circle into 40 segments. Mark 1 line "Start" and "Finish." Label remaining segments from 500 to 19,500 as shown. Divide the inner part of each circle into 16 segments.
5. Use the felt-tip pens to write in the names of the largest U.S. cities (shown at the right), one in each segment.
6. For players' reference, provide a map of the U.S., with distance scale or a standard table showing land or airline distances between U.S. cities.

HOW TO PLAY *(2 teams of 2 players each)*

1. Each team of two players operates one of the spinners and "travels" on the outside track of its spinner.
2. Each team puts its marker at the Start point on the outside track of its spinner.
3. Team 1 takes the first turn. Both teams spin their spinners. Each pointer stops and indicates a city. Team 1 uses the map or reference table to find the distance between these two cities. The marker for Team 1 is then moved that distance forward on its track.
4. Each team, in turn, continues in this way until one team wins by completing the entire distance (20,000 miles) around the track.

Circle 1	Circle 2
New York, NY	Philadelphia, PA
Chicago, IL	San Diego, CA
Los Angeles, CA	San Antonio, TX
Houston, TX	Phoenix, AZ
Detroit, MI	San Francisco, CA
Dallas, TX	San Jose, CA
Baltimore, MD	Jacksonville, FL
Indianapolis, IN	Seattle, WA
Honolulu, HI	Denver, CO
Washington, DC	Kansas City, MO
Memphis, TN	Pittsburgh, PA
Milwaukee, WI	Nashville, TN
Boston, MA	Atlanta, GA
New Orleans, LA	Cincinnati, OH
Columbus, OH	Toledo, OH
St. Louis, MO	Buffalo, NY

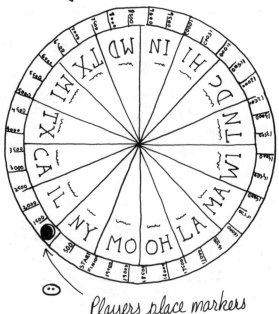

Write in names on each segment of circle.

Players place markers in this track.

60

Recycled Junk Games

Think twice before you throw away that cereal box, tin can, or cardboard paper tube—there could be weeks of fun in them. Here are games made from stuff salvaged from the trash heap and a few additional household items.

Tube-A-Loopa

Players need quick observation and calculation skills to keep track of the game ball as it goes into one scoring hole and, possibly, out another.

MATERIALS AND TOOLS

Cardboard box, about 2 inches deep, 9 inches wide, and 12 inches long (a shirt box is ideal)
Scissors
6 cardboard tubes from rolls of toilet tissue
Stapler
White glue
Felt-tip pen
Large marble or rubber ball

CONSTRUCTION

1. Remove the top of the cardboard box and completely cut out one end panel.
2. On the bottom of the box, cut down the two corners at one end so that the panel can be bent down flat.
3. Check to see that six toilet tissue tubes fit neatly into the 9-inch sides of the box. If the fit is good, put the tubes on a flat surface and staple them together side by side to make sure they stay flat. If there is space left over, staple them in two groups of three.
4. Apply ample stripes of glue to the sides and bottoms of the cardboard tubes. Set the tubes in the bottom of the box, just even with the sides at the open end. If the tubes fit with room to spare, rearrange the tubes so that the open space is in the middle.
5. Put the box top back on and mark numerical values of 5, 10, 15, 20, 10, and 5 above each tube opening.

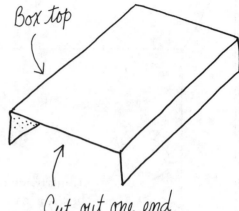

Box top

Cut out one end.

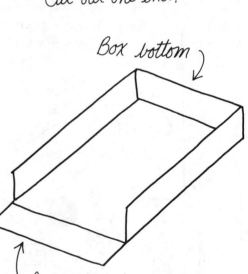

Box bottom

Cut down the corners of one end. Fold out as shown.

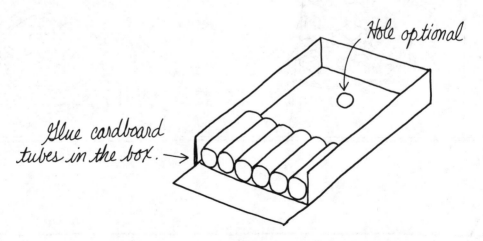

Hole optional

Glue cardboard tubes in the box. →

62

HOW TO PLAY *(2 to 4 players)*

1. Play on a smooth floor or a long table. Set the closed end of the Tube-A-Loopa box on a book so that it tilts down toward the players. Find a large marble or a small rubber ball for rolling.
2. Each player has one roll per turn. To figure the score, multiply the value of the tube the ball goes in by the value of the tube the ball comes out. For example, if the ball goes in the 5 tube and comes out the 10 tube, the score is 50.
3. The first player to score 1,000 wins the game.

■ VARIATIONS

1. Try adding an element of risk by cutting a 1-inch hole in the bottom of the box about 3 inches from the closed end. The player whose ball drops through this hole loses half of his or her total score.
2. Try changing the numerical values of the tubes to numbers like 7, 33, 58, 13, 4, and 12, rather than multiples of 5. This makes the multiplication a tougher challenge.

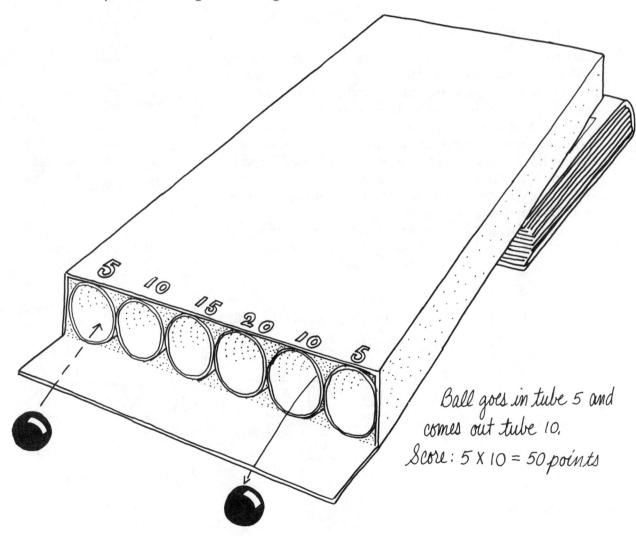

Ball goes in tube 5 and comes out tube 10.
Score: 5 × 10 = 50 points

Tiddly Wink Croquet

This game, in which players make words out of letter cards, can be a snap. All it takes is good aim, carefully planned moves, some word skills, and a little luck on the draw.

MATERIALS AND TOOLS

8 empty tuna or cat food cans, 6½- or 7-ounce size
Scissors
Sheet of paper, 8½ inches wide and 11 inches long
Felt-tip pen
Full set of Letter Cards (Game Sheet #12 on page 88)
Can opener
Large flat buttons or plastic chips, 2 for each player

CONSTRUCTION

1. Make sure to remove the tops of the tin cans cleanly, leaving no burrs or sharp edges that can cause cuts. Also, remove the bottoms of four of the cans, using a good can opener and again making sure there are no sharp spots.
2. Make a wicket by setting one of the open-ended cans sideways into one of the topless cans. Make three more.
3. Arrange the wickets about 12–18 inches apart in a diamond shape on a flat surface.
4. Mark a big X on the sheet of paper and place it in the middle of the diamond playing area.
5. Duplicate and cut out the Letter Cards. Put about one-fourth of the Letter Cards into the bottom can of each wicket.

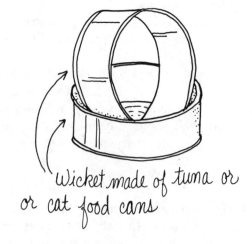

Wicket made of tuna or or cat food cans

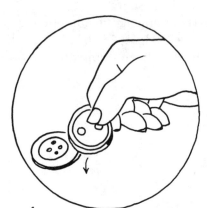

Snap down to propel the wink.

a player whose button snaps through the wicket draws 6 cards.

B O A T
I C

HOW TO PLAY *(2 to 4 players)*

1. Beginning at wicket 1, players snap one button to propel the other button, much like Tiddley Winks. The object of the game is to snap a button through wickets 1, 2, and 3, back through 3, on through 4, and finally up into 1.

2. If a player's button (or "wink") goes *into* a wicket when it's supposed to go *through,* the player moves the button to the X position in the middle of the diamond area. From there, the player again aims for the same wicket. Each player gets one snap per turn.

3. A player who snaps through a wicket then draws six Letter Cards, without looking, from the bottom of the wicket.

4. The player must then make a word using four or more of the cards.

5. If the player makes a word, he or she returns the cards to the bottom of the wicket and takes an extra turn.

6. If the player cannot make a word from the cards drawn, he or she holds on to the cards and moves the wink to the X position. From there, the player must again proceed to the same wicket. Once through the wicket, the player draws six more cards and again tries to make a word.

7. The first player to get through all wickets and to snap the wink into the first wicket is the winner.

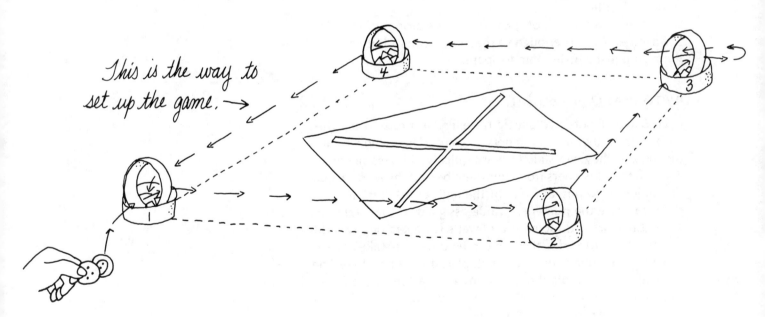

This is the way to set up the game. →

Snap Shots

Players test their multiplication and plastic-fastener-snapping skills as they shoot for top scores. Who can shoot through the front rows to reach the high numbers? Take good aim and find out!

MATERIALS AND TOOLS

Plywood ½ inch thick, 8 inches wide, and 12 inches long
Ruler
Felt-tip pen
18 finish nails, 1½ inches long
Hammer
6 flat plastic fasteners (from bread or food bags)
Scissors

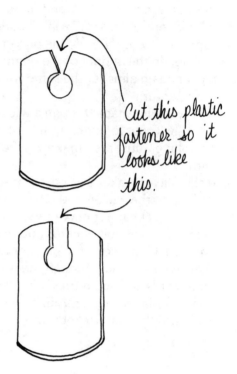

Cut this plastic fastener so it looks like this.

CONSTRUCTION

1. Measure and mark positions for nails on the plywood, as shown in the diagram. Mark numbers, ranging from 25 to 200, on the board. Mark the starting line.
2. Hammer nails into the board just deep enough so that they stand up firmly.
3. Using the scissors, snip off just a bit of the prongs of the plastic fastener. Cut off enough so that a nail can fit between them with just a little room to spare.

HOW TO PLAY *(2 to 4 players)*

1. Each player shoots five plastic fasteners at a turn, using the sixth to snap the other fasteners forward. (They won't fly in the air, but they will slide forward quickly.) Players place and aim their fasteners from anywhere behind the starting line. The object is to ring any one of the nails or "stakes" in order to score the numerical value assigned to that stake.
2. The total score is doubled if a player's fasteners ring two different stakes, tripled if they ring three different stakes, quadrupled if they ring four, and quintupled if they ring five. The total score is multiplied by 10 if any two fasteners are snapped onto the same stake.
3. The first player to score 3,000 wins.

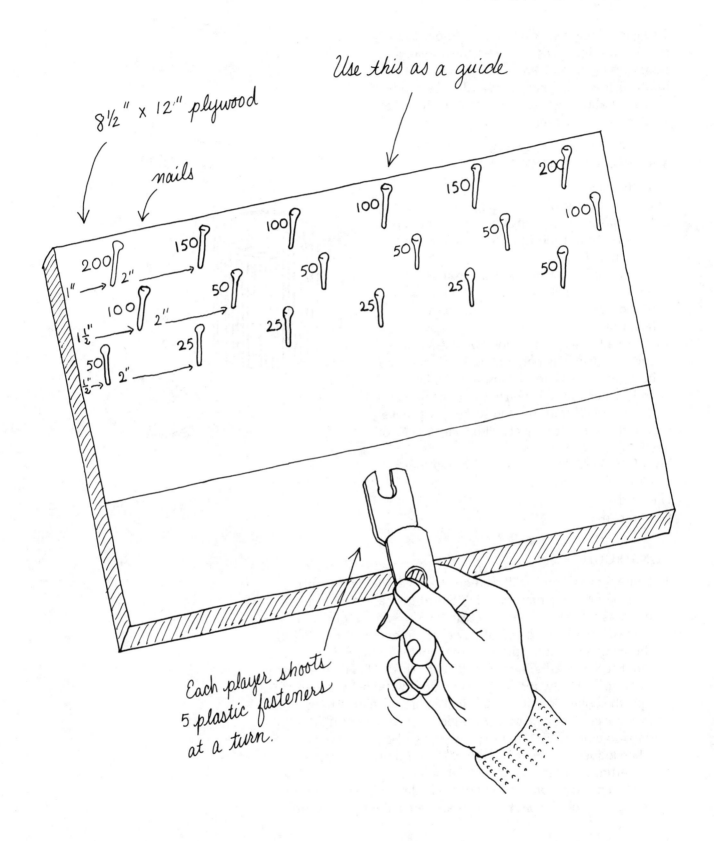

Use this as a guide

8½" x 12" plywood

nails

200 ⏐ 2" → 150 ⏐   100 ⏐   100 ⏐   150 ⏐   200 ⏐

1" →   50 ⏐   50 ⏐   50 ⏐   100 ⏐

100 ⏐ 2" → 50 ⏐   50 ⏐   25 ⏐   50 ⏐

1½" →   25 ⏐   25 ⏐

50 ⏐ 2" → 25 ⏐

½" →

Each player shoots
5 plastic fasteners
at a turn.

Think or Sink

This game takes two kinds of know-how: factual knowledge, so that players can answer questions in learning areas such as vocabulary, math, history and geography; and some good judgment about the weight and "sinkability" of small objects in water.

MATERIALS AND TOOLS

2 empty cans
Towel or paper toweling
2 deep plastic bottle caps (the kind found on large bottles of mouthwash, shampoo, or other liquids)
2 coins or metal washers that fit exactly into the bottoms of the bottle caps (a nickel will fit most smaller caps, and a quarter will fit larger ones)
25–50 small objects of various weights, shapes, and sizes (such as paper clips; small nuts and bolts; dried peas and beans; metal, plastic, and rubber washers; pencil top erasers; plastic and metal buttons; and so on—just make sure there are no objects with sharp points or edges)
List of 25–50 spelling words or fact questions with correct answers
File cards
Felt-tip pen

Put coin or washer in cap bottom.

CONSTRUCTION

1. Some trial and error will be required to get the right combination of playing materials. Fill one of the cans about three-quarters full with water for a test. Put the can on some old newspaper and have a small towel or paper towels handy for the small amount of splashing that goes with the game.
2. Put a coin or washer into a bottle cap. This will keep the cap floating perfectly upright so that it doesn't tip on its side.
3. Test the collection of small objects, placing them into the floating cap to make sure the added weight won't sink the cap too quickly. But make sure that it will eventually sink when loaded with many of the objects. Adjust, if necessary, by getting smaller caps or heavier objects.
4. Write a question on the front of each file card. Write the correct answer on the back. These cards are called Think Cards.

HOW TO PLAY *(2 players)*

1. Each player fills a can three-quarters full of water and places a bottle cap in it so that it floats. The bottle caps are weighted with a coin or washer. The collection of small objects is placed between the two players. The deck of Think Cards is set faceup in the middle.

2. Flip a coin to see who goes first. The first player draws a card and reads the opponent the spelling word or fact question written on it. The opponent offers what he or she thinks is the correct spelling or answer. The first player checks the back of the card. If the opponent's answer is correct, he or she may choose any one item from the collection and place it carefully (no dropping or throwing allowed) in the first player's floating cap. If the answer is incorrect, the opponent must choose an item and place it in his or her own floating cap.

3. The player whose cap sinks to the bottom of the can first loses the game.

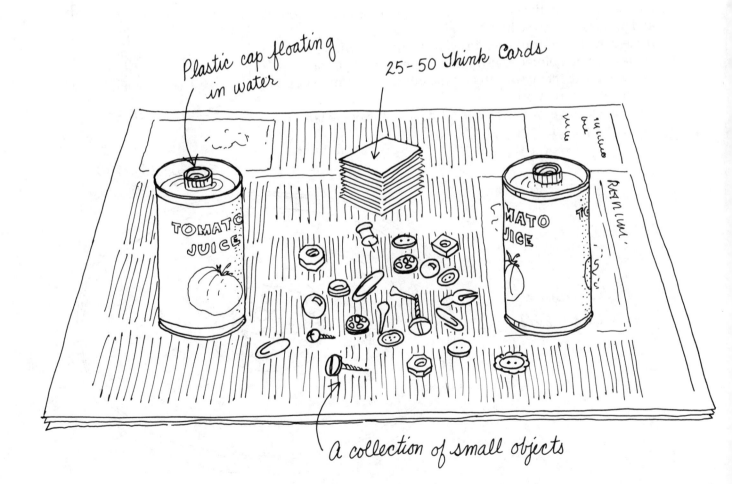

Plastic cap floating in water

25-50 Think Cards

a collection of small objects

Pasta Word Pour

Letters and numbers are the main elements in this game, which challenges players' vocabulary, spelling, and calculation skills. A lucky pour can help the player get very high scores.

MATERIALS AND TOOLS

Cardboard bread crumb canister with spout on side, 8-ounce size
Punch-type can opener
1/4 pound of alphabet pasta
4 plastic container lids, 4 inches in diameter, preferably any color but white
4 metal beverage bottle caps
4 pencils

CONSTRUCTION

1. Punch a triangular hole in the top of the canister exactly opposite the spout.
2. Put the pasta into the canister by slowly pouring it on the top and pushing it into the hole.
3. If the only plastic container lids you can find are white, glue circles of dark-colored construction paper onto their tops. This will make the pasta letters stand out more. Colored lids can be used as they are.
4. Equip each player with a plastic lid, a metal beverage bottle cap, and a pencil.

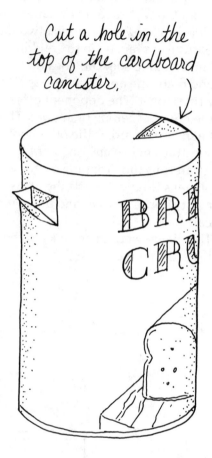

Cut a hole in the top of the cardboard canister.

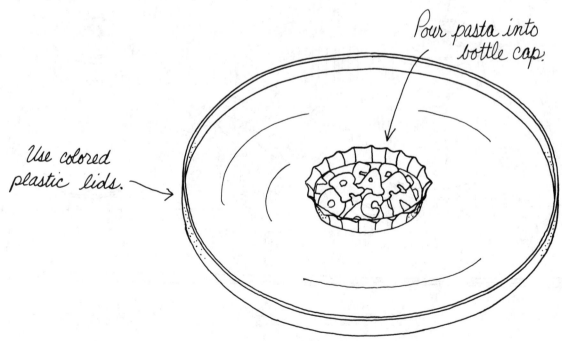

Pour pasta into bottle cap.

Use colored plastic lids.

HOW TO PLAY *(4 players)*

1. Players place the bottle caps in the center of their plastic lid. Each player pours pasta letters and numbers from the canister spout into the bottle cap. Enough letters and numbers should be poured to half-fill the cap.

2. At the start signal, players dump the contents of the cap onto the lid. Players first separate letters and numbers, and then form as many words as they can from the letters. Players use their fingers or their pencils to move the pasta pieces.

3. The recommended time limit for each round is three minutes. If all the players agree, this limit may be lengthened or shortened.

4. No more than 20 pasta pieces may be used for the final word and number count. If the player has used more than 20 pieces, the extra pieces must be pushed aside before the score is calculated.

5. Score 1 point for each letter in each word formed by a player. Score 1 bonus point for a word of six or more letters.

6. All number pasta—1 through 8— are added together. (Don't count 9s as 9; they're just upside down 6s.) The total number points are then multiplied by the total word points for the final round score. In the round illustrated here, the player has 11 word points, multiplied by 23 number points, for a total score of 253.

7. Play continues until one player wins with a score of 1,000.

11   word points
23   number points
_____
11 × 23 = 253 *points for round*

Roller Sentences

A big tin becomes a rolling word grid, collecting magnetic bits in its path. The magnetic bits point out what words the player can use in an attempt to make the best and longest complete sentences.

MATERIALS AND TOOLS

Plastic strip magnet, as small as ¹/₂ inch by 1 inch
Scissors
Large brown paper bag
Ruler
Black felt-tip pen
Fruit can, 46-ounce size, 13 inches in circumference, 7 inches high

CONSTRUCTION

1. Use the scissors to snip eight very small pieces of plastic magnet, about ¹/₈ inch wide and ¹/₂ inch long.
2. From an unseamed and unmarked part of the brown paper bag, cut a piece exactly 14 inches long and 6⁵/₈ inches wide.
3. Use the ruler and the felt-tip pen to mark the length of the brown paper into 1-inch columns. Leave the column at the right end blank (it will be overlapped when it's wrapped around the tin can). Divide the other columns into six 1-inch blocks and one ⁵/₈-inch block at the bottom.
4. Write the 91 words listed at the right at random onto the grid, one to a block.
5. Wrap the paper grid tightly around the can, making sure that the unmarked end portion of the paper is the portion that is overlapped. Use strips of cellophane tape to secure the paper to the can.

Word list for the grid →

a	him
a	his
a	house
about	I
about	I
and	laughed
and	lion
at	mean
at	mother
ate	of
ball	of
because	or
blue	our
book	played
boy	pretty
brave	ran
but	read
by	red
car	sad
cat	said
chewed	saw
class	school
coach	she
color	smart
cried	teacher
dog	television
dreamed	the
elephant	the
father	the
forgot	the
free	their
free	their
free	they
free	thought
free	to
free	to
free	tried
from	us
game	walked
girl	we
great	yelled
happy	yellow
have	you
he	you
her	your
her	

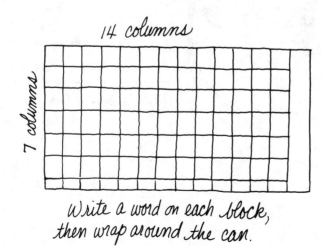

14 columns

7 columns

Write a word on each block, then wrap around the can.

HOW TO PLAY

1. The game is played on a hard flat tabletop or floor area at least 3 feet long and 2 feet wide. Mark the limits with chalk or string. Players take their places at the ends of the playing area, facing each other.
2. The first player places the eight small magnet pieces down on the playing surface. The pieces may be placed anywhere, but they must be at least 1 inch away from each other and at least 6 inches from the sides of the playing surface.
3. The second player rolls the can twice so that it can pick up the magnetic pieces.
4. The player who rolled the can then picks it up to see what words have magnetic pieces stuck to them. If a piece touches two blocks, the player may use the words in both blocks. The word *free* may be used to represent itself or any other word the player chooses.
5. The player makes the longest sentence possible from the words marked by the magnetic pieces. Score 1 for each word in a proper sentence. (Sentences may be nonsensical as long as they are grammatically correct.)
6. Players continue, in turn, until one wins with a score of 25 points.

Can picks up the magnets.

■ VARIATIONS

1. Players keep and list all the words they get, using them from turn to turn to make sentences.
2. Fill the grid with facts from various categories in literature, math, science, or social studies. For example, include: titles of books or poems by various authors; prime numbers, fractions, or decimal fractions; animals, vegetables, or minerals; and countries, rivers, or bodies of water. After the players roll, they check to see which grid items have magnetic bits stuck to them. They categorize the items, and for every item over four in any category, score 1 point. The first player to score 25 wins.

Playing area 2 ft. × 3 ft. Mark area with chalk or string.

Magnets

Player rolls can over the magnets.

WORDS HIT: LAUGHED, A , YELLED, RAN, HER, OF, BRAVE, FREE, AND, ATE, HE

SENTENCE: HE ATE HER BRAVE CAR AND LAUGHED.

SCORE: *7 points*

Blizzard

With their snowblowers, players develop physical skills and a sense of math ideas such as trajectory and air pressure. What strategy scores best? High floaters or low drives? Small flurries or one big storm? Try them all.

MATERIALS AND TOOLS

6–8 empty tin cans, ranging in size from tuna fish cans to large juice cans
Felt-tip pen
Cellophane tape and scraps of paper, or gummed labels
Soup can, 10½-ounce size
30 Styrofoam "peanuts" or nut-sized Styrofoam chunks

CONSTRUCTION

1. Label each of the containers except the 10½-ounce can with a point value ranging from 10 to 100. Give the lowest value to the container with the widest mouth, and the highest value to the container with the narrowest mouth. Cluster the containers to make the target.

HOW TO PLAY (2 to 4 players)

1. Place the 30 Styrofoam peanuts in the 10½-ounce can. Each player stands at least two feet from the target cluster of containers, but may move farther back and shoot from a standing, kneeling, or sitting position.
2. Each player holds the snowblower can at a slightly upward angle and blows against the far inside edge of the can. This causes the Styrofoam pieces to fly like snow out of the can toward the target. Players may blow the pieces out in small flurries or in one big blizzard.
3. A player's score is determined by the point value on each can in which a peanut lands. The first player to get 100 points wins.

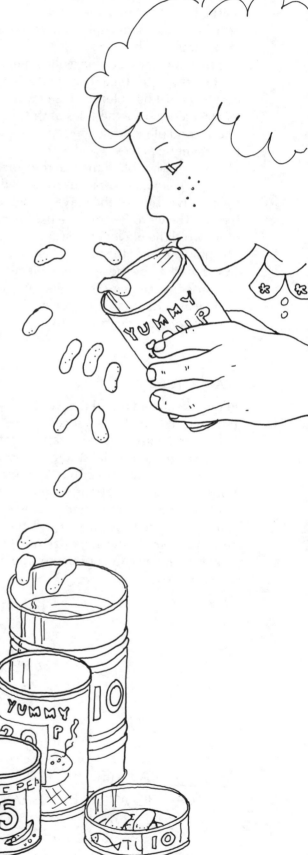

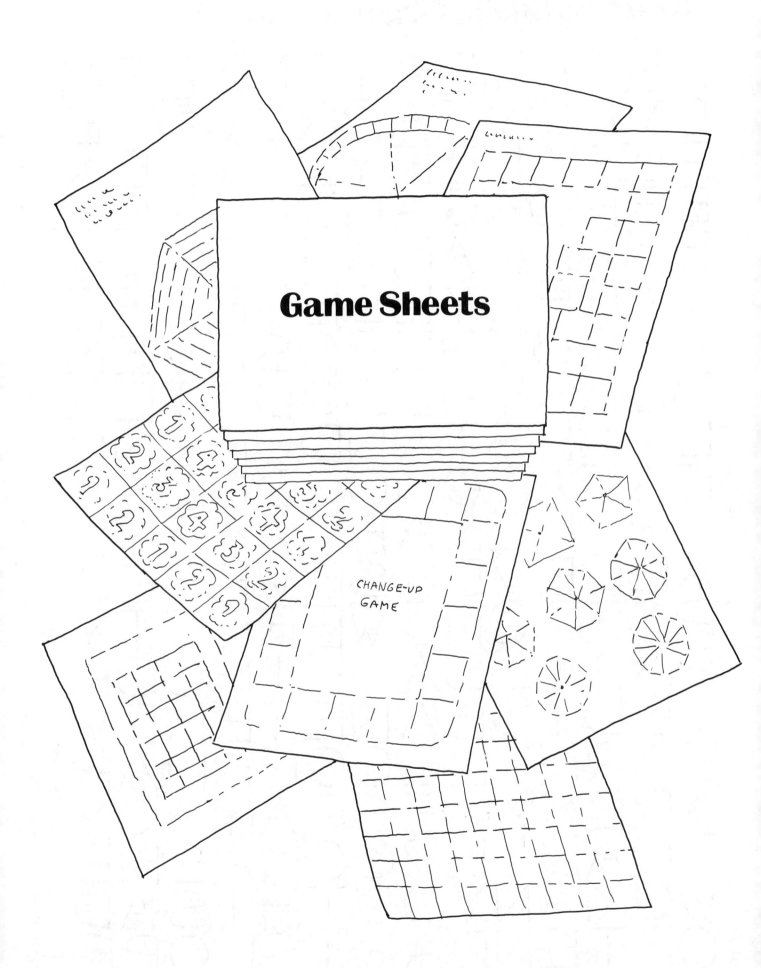

Word Find Quoits Target

```
R E A C H E A T E N T E N T E R M
O V E R Y E A R R O W D Y E
P E T A L L E Y E T I D E N
E R R O R G A N D E N Y E S
S M A L L A M A G I C A G E
T A P P L Y E S E T H E R E
A I L O T H E R O S E V E N
B L A R E A L S O D A T E A
L I N E S T A N D U P E N D
E A T A T O M O O D D E A R
T R I P E N A B R A K E Y E
A B L E V E R S E W E R E D
P O E T C H E W E R E S T Y
P R A Y E S A I L I P O O R
L E D I D E A N E T E N E W
E A R N I L E G G E R M A R
A R E G A L E S P A N I C Y
T O A D Z E R O O M A S H E
W O M A N Y O U T H I S A D
O F T E N D A R T S L O P E
```

Word Scramble Quoits Target GAME SHEET #2

```
C  O  I  Y  G  O      M  E     U
   S     T  B  L  F      M  E  U     E  Y
   L  U  O  E  I  N     R  A  R  D  D     S
      C  I  L  D  N  E  B  O  K     V
         T  H  O  N  E  D  N     E     W
      W  P  E  T  G  Z  E  D     D  T  E
      T  A  K  R  I  G  Z  E  D     R  A
      L  N  M  A  E  V  M  A  E     P
         C  E  A  C  V  O  E  S  T  Y
         L  A  Y  Z  D  R  Y  S  A
         A  S  H  R  B     V  E  K
            P  U  T  A     B  T  E  F
               T  R  E  O  A  E  O  R
               S  A  I  D  B  Y  U  L
                     E  N  R  S  A  H  E
```

Make Your Own Games Workshop. Copyright © 1982

Number Quoits Target GAME SHEET #3

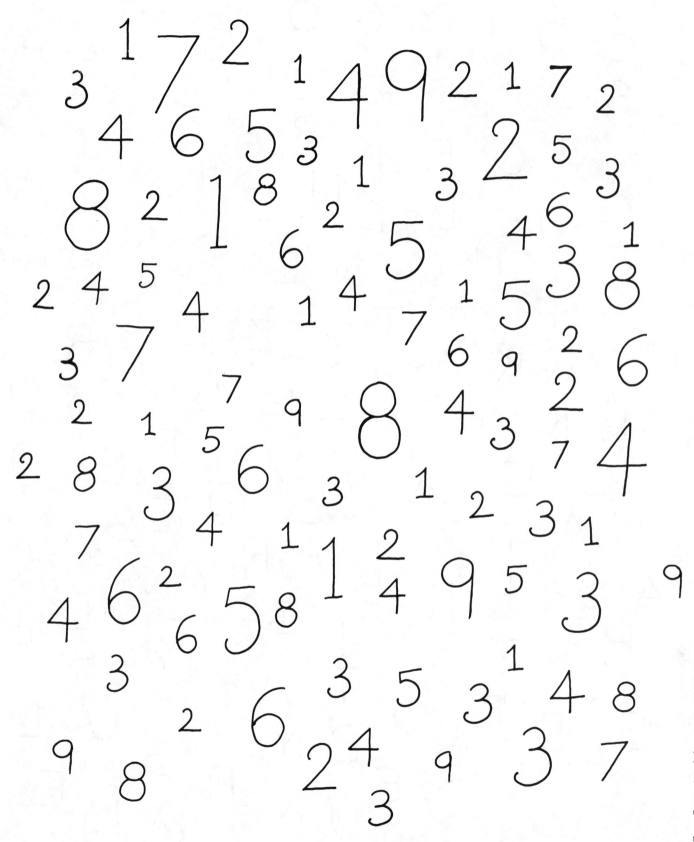

Make Your Own Games Workshop. Copyright © 1982

Hexagon Pattern GAME SHEET #4

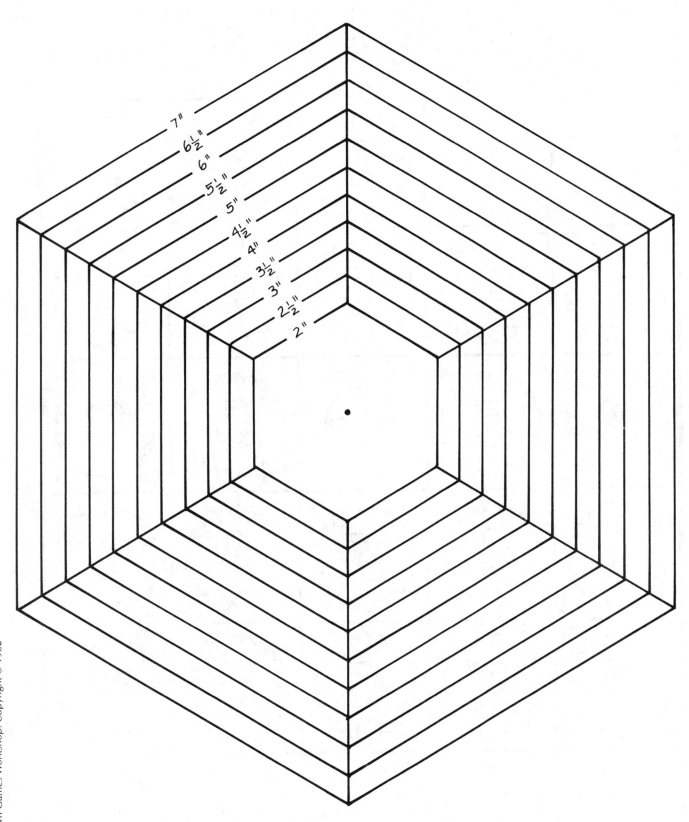

7"
6½"
6"
5½"
5"
4½"
4"
3½"
3"
2½"
2"

Make Your Own Games Workshop. Copyright © 1982

Spin Skittle Number Pattern GAME SHEET #5

1	2	1	2	1
2	3	4	3	2
1	4	5	4	1
2	5	⊕	5	2
1	4	5	4	1
2	3	4	3	2
1	2	1	2	1

Make Your Own Games Workshop. Copyright © 1982

Teetotum Spinner Patterns GAME SHEET #6

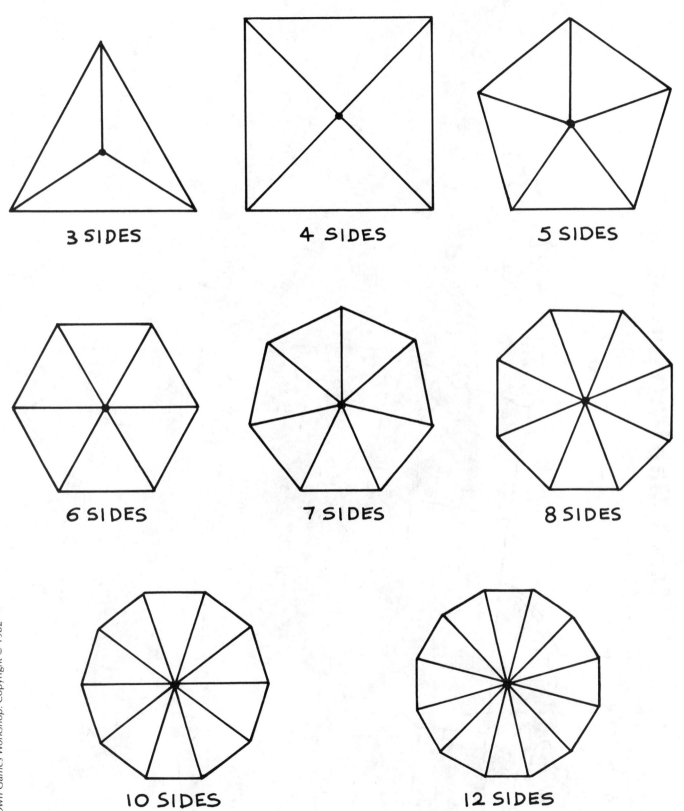

3 SIDES

4 SIDES

5 SIDES

6 SIDES

7 SIDES

8 SIDES

10 SIDES

12 SIDES

Make Your Own Games Workshop. Copyright © 1982

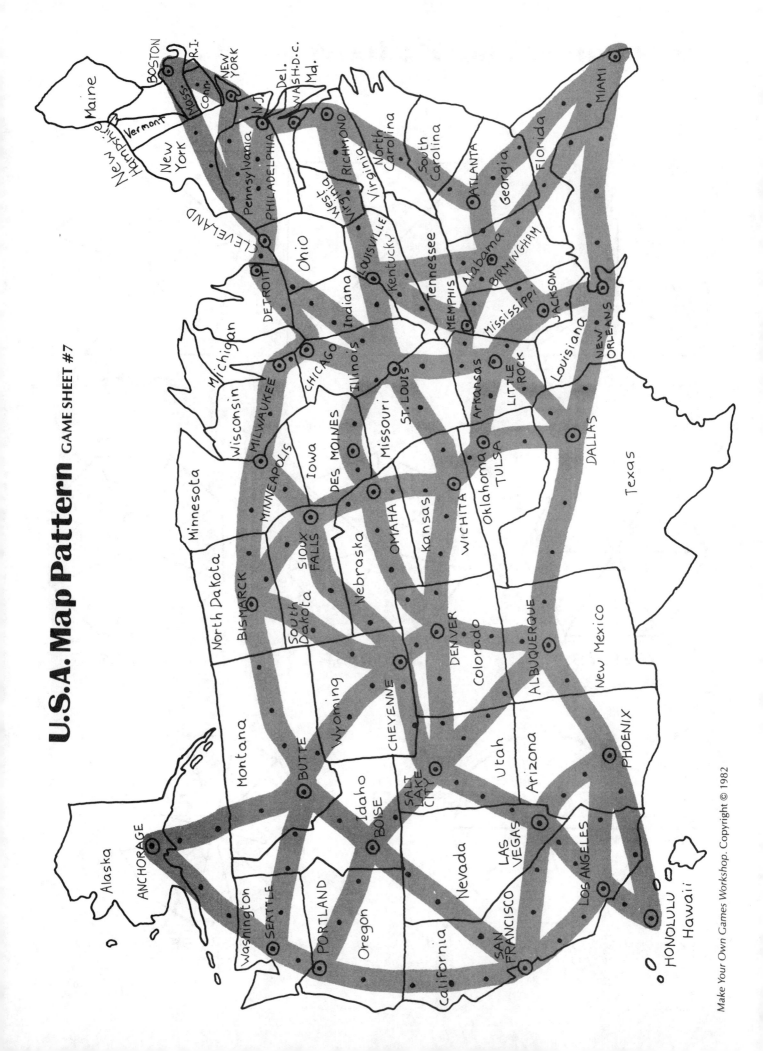

U.S.A. Map Pattern GAME SHEET #7

Make Your Own Games Workshop. Copyright © 1982

Animal Hunt Pattern GAME SHEET #8

ARMADILLO	BEAR	BEAVER	BUFFALO	CAMEL
CHIPMUNK	COW	DEER	DOG	DONKEY
ELEPHANT	FOX	GIRAFFE	GOAT	HORSE
KANGAROO	KOALA	ANIMAL HUNT	LEOPARD	LION
LLAMA	MINK	MOOSE	OPOSSUM	PIG
PORCUPINE	RABBIT	RACCOON	RHINOCEROS	SHEEP
SKUNK	SQUIRREL	TIGER	WOLF	WOODCHUCK

Make Your Own Games Workshop. Copyright © 1982

Shopping List Pattern GAME SHEET #9

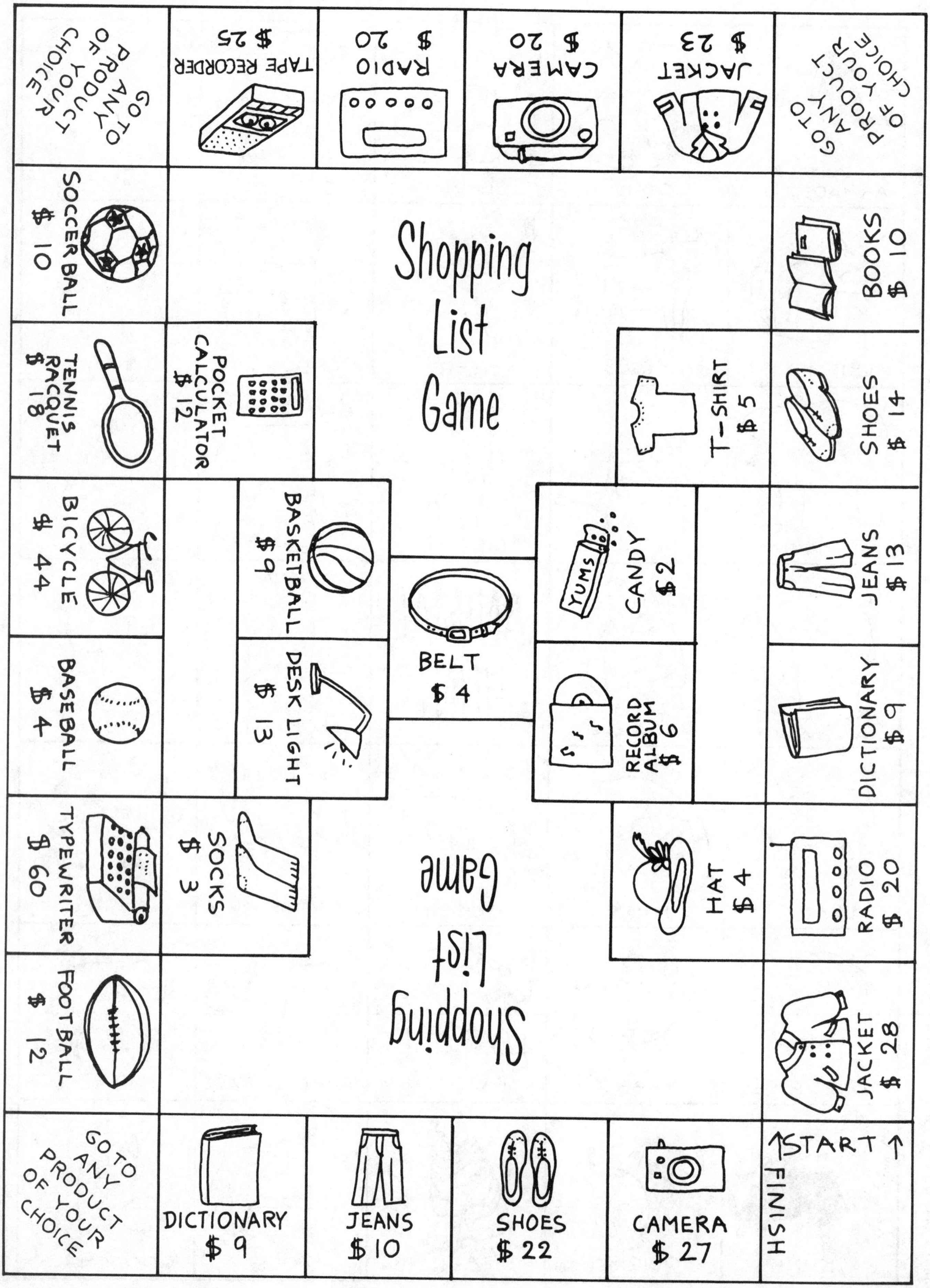

Shopping List Game

GO TO ANY PRODUCT OF YOUR CHOICE

TAPE RECORDER $ 25

RADIO $ 20

CAMERA $ 20

JACKET $ 23

GO TO ANY PRODUCT OF YOUR CHOICE

SOCCER BALL $ 10

BOOKS $ 10

TENNIS RACQUET $ 18

POCKET CALCULATOR $ 12

T-SHIRT $ 5

SHOES $ 14

BICYCLE $ 44

BASKETBALL $ 9

CANDY $ 2
YUMS

JEANS $ 13

BELT $ 4

BASEBALL $ 4

DESK LIGHT $ 13

RECORD ALBUM $ 6

DICTIONARY $ 9

TYPEWRITER $ 60

SOCKS $ 3

HAT $ 4

RADIO $ 20

FOOTBALL $ 12

Shopping List Game

JACKET $ 28

GO TO ANY PRODUCT OF YOUR CHOICE

DICTIONARY $ 9

JEANS $ 10

SHOES $ 22

CAMERA $ 27

↑ START ↑

FINISH

Make Your Own Games Workshop. Copyright © 1982

Remember Pattern GAME SHEET #10

START →

| 1 | 8 | 2 | 4 | 7 | 3 | 6 | 9 | 5 | 0 | 3 | 1 | 5 | 7 | 2 |

REMEMBER

0														8
2		1	6	7		1	8	0		8	7	8		4
9		5		9		9		7		9		7		9
1		0		4		5		0		4		8		0
8		5		6		3		2		5		3		6
1		7		2		8		4		3		4		1
3		3		4		1		2		5		6		3
8		3		8		1		7		4		4		4
2		2		6		6		3		6		1		1
0		9		3		1		3		2		5		5
9		4		9		2		9		9		1		2
7		6		7		8		2		6		2		6
4		0		4		0		3		5		7		2
0		2		2		5		0		0		0		7
9		1		3		4		4		8		8		4
5		5		6		5		3		6		0		8
1		7		6		8		5		9		6		3
8	2	6		3	7	1		9	1	7		7	9	5

Make Your Own Games Workshop. Copyright © 1982

CHANGE-UP
GAME

Make Your Own Games Workshop. Copyright © 1982

Boxing Match

	1	2	3	4	5
A					
B					
C					
D					
E					

Make Your Own Games Workshop. Copyright © 1982

Letter Cards GAME SHEET #13

E	E	E	E	E	E	E	E	E	E
T	T	T	T	T	T	T	T	T	Z
M	A	A	A	A	A	A	A	A	M
M	O	O	O	O	O	O	O	P	M
M	N	N	N	N	N	N	P	P	F
P	F	I	I	I	I	I	I	I	F
P	F	R	R	R	R	R	R	W	Y
P	Y	S	S	S	S	S	S	W	G
Y	W	H	H	H	H	H	H	G	B
W	G	D	D	D	D	D	D	B	V
G	B	L	L	L	L	L	L	V	J
B	V	U	U	U	U	U	U	J	K	K
J	K	C	C	C	C	C	C	Q	Q	X

Make Your Own Games Workshop. Copyright © 1982

Cover-Up Pattern GAME SHEET #14

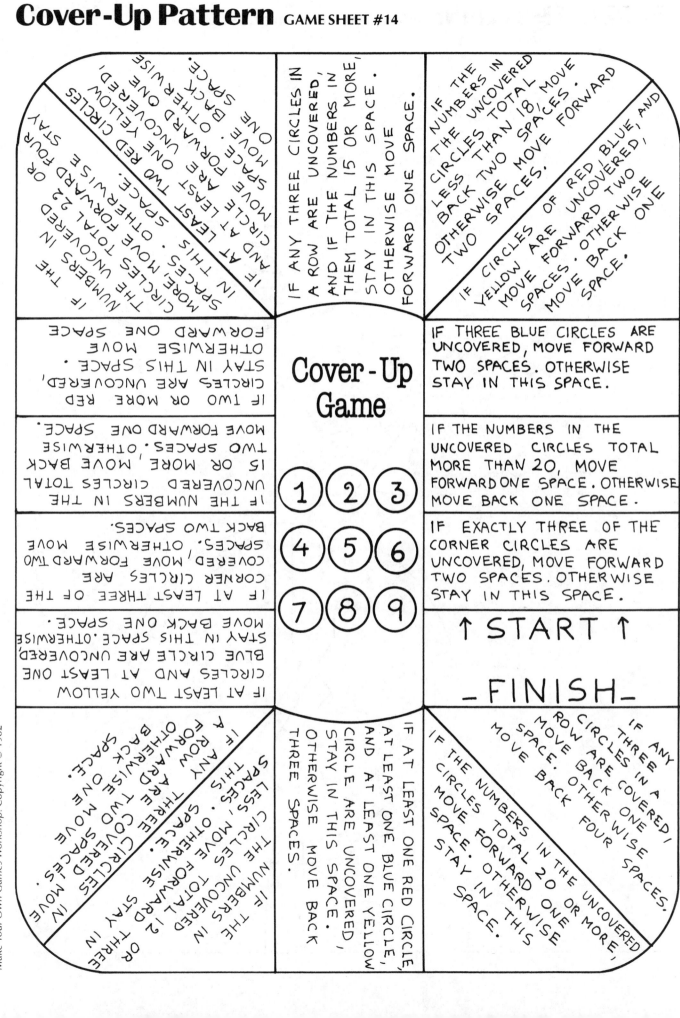

Cover-Up Game

① ② ③
④ ⑤ ⑥
⑦ ⑧ ⑨

IF ANY THREE CIRCLES IN A ROW ARE UNCOVERED, AND IF THE NUMBERS IN THEM TOTAL 15 OR MORE, STAY IN THIS SPACE. OTHERWISE MOVE FORWARD ONE SPACE.

IF THE NUMBERS IN THE UNCOVERED CIRCLES TOTAL LESS THAN 18, MOVE BACK TWO SPACES. OTHERWISE MOVE FORWARD TWO SPACES.

IF CIRCLES OF RED, BLUE, AND YELLOW ARE UNCOVERED, MOVE FORWARD TWO SPACES. OTHERWISE MOVE BACK ONE SPACE.

IF THREE BLUE CIRCLES ARE UNCOVERED, MOVE FORWARD TWO SPACES. OTHERWISE STAY IN THIS SPACE.

IF THE NUMBERS IN THE UNCOVERED CIRCLES TOTAL MORE THAN 20, MOVE FORWARD ONE SPACE. OTHERWISE MOVE BACK ONE SPACE.

IF EXACTLY THREE OF THE CORNER CIRCLES ARE UNCOVERED, MOVE FORWARD TWO SPACES. OTHERWISE STAY IN THIS SPACE.

↑ START ↑

— FINISH —

IF THE NUMBERS IN THE UNCOVERED CIRCLES TOTAL 20 OR MORE, MOVE FORWARD ONE SPACE. OTHERWISE STAY IN THIS SPACE.

IF ANY THREE CIRCLES IN A ROW ARE COVERED, MOVE BACK ONE SPACE. OTHERWISE MOVE BACK FOUR SPACES.

IF AT LEAST ONE RED CIRCLE, AT LEAST ONE BLUE CIRCLE, AND AT LEAST ONE YELLOW CIRCLE ARE UNCOVERED, STAY IN THIS SPACE. OTHERWISE MOVE BACK THREE SPACES.

IF THE NUMBERS IN THE UNCOVERED CIRCLES TOTAL 12 OR LESS, MOVE FORWARD THREE SPACES. OTHERWISE STAY IN THIS SPACE.

IF ANY THREE CIRCLES IN A ROW ARE COVERED, MOVE FORWARD TWO SPACES. OTHERWISE MOVE BACK ONE SPACE.

IF AT LEAST TWO YELLOW CIRCLES AND AT LEAST ONE BLUE CIRCLE ARE UNCOVERED, STAY IN THIS SPACE. OTHERWISE MOVE BACK ONE SPACE.

IF AT LEAST THREE OF THE CORNER CIRCLES ARE COVERED, MOVE FORWARD TWO SPACES. OTHERWISE MOVE BACK TWO SPACES.

IF THE NUMBERS IN THE UNCOVERED CIRCLES TOTAL 15 OR MORE, MOVE BACK TWO SPACES. OTHERWISE MOVE FORWARD ONE SPACE.

IF TWO OR MORE RED CIRCLES ARE UNCOVERED, STAY IN THIS SPACE. OTHERWISE MOVE FORWARD ONE SPACE

IF THE NUMBERS IN THE UNCOVERED CIRCLES TOTAL 20 OR MORE, MOVE FORWARD TWO SPACES. OTHERWISE STAY IN THIS SPACE. IF AT LEAST TWO RED CIRCLES ARE UNCOVERED, MOVE FORWARD ONE SPACE. OTHERWISE MOVE BACK ONE SPACE.

Make Your Own Games Workshop. Copyright © 1982

Spinner Pattern

Use this pattern to make spinner circles with a number
of segments up to 20. Follow these steps:

1. Duplicate the pattern.
2. Choose the number of segments desired. Locate the cor-
   responding number wherever it appears outside the circle and
   draw lines from those points to the center of the circle.
3. Glue the pattern onto a piece of cardboard.
4. Cut out the circle.

Make Your Own Games Workshop. Copyright © 1982

Spinner Pattern GAME SHEET #15

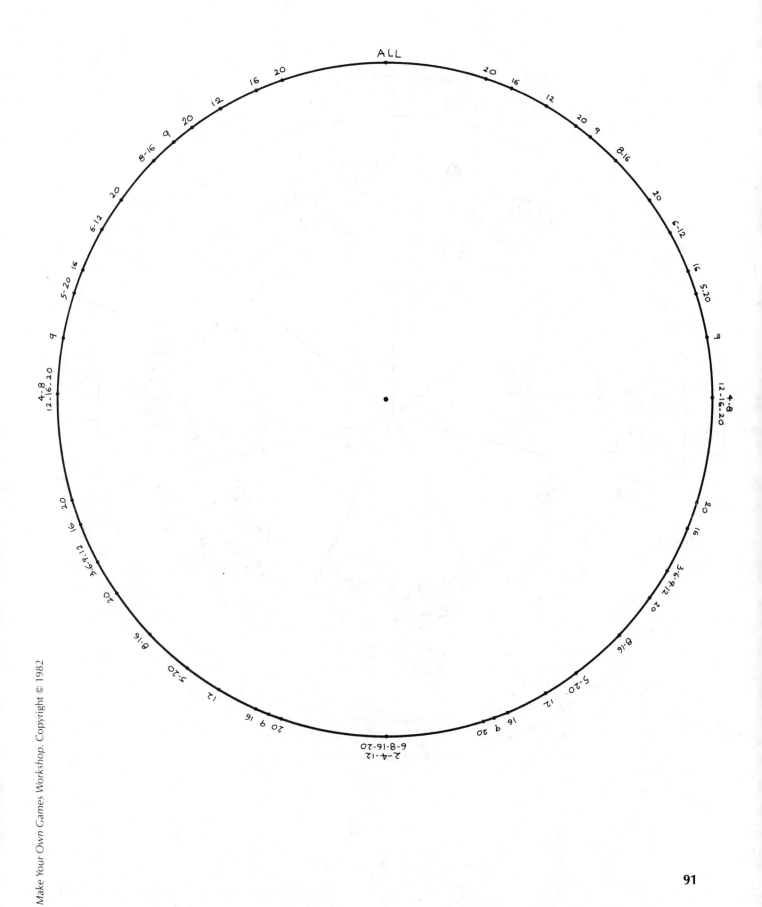

Make Your Own Games Workshop. Copyright © 1982

Parts of Speech Circle GAME SHEET #16

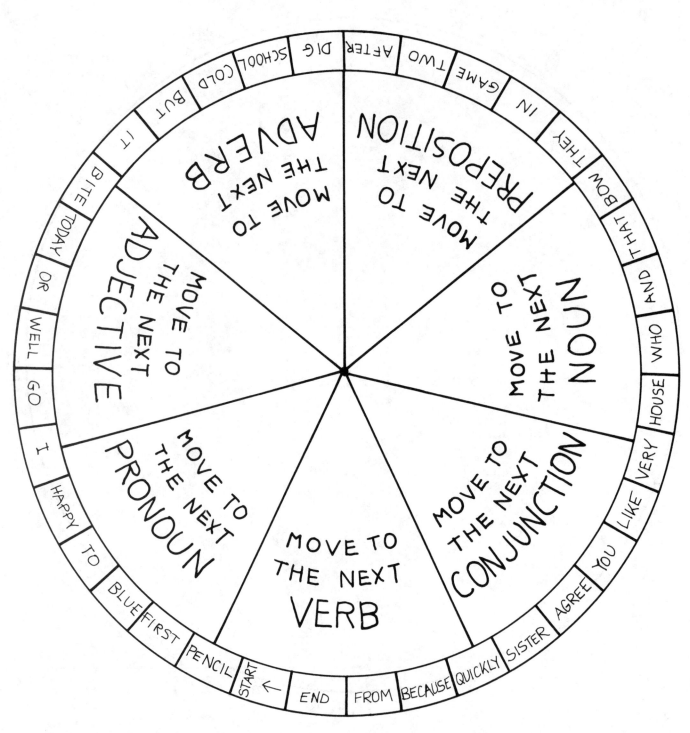

Make Your Own Games Workshop. Copyright © 1982